Human Security
in an Insecure World

by
John Grayzel

Dialogue contributions by
Patrick Cronin
Kishan Manocha
Mishkat al-Moumin
Constance Newman

Edited with an annotated bibliography by
Michael Dravis

Falls Church, VA: Dialogue & Consultation Press, 2011

HUMAN SECURITY IN AN INSECURE WORLD

ISBN-13: 978-0-9836088-0-6
ISBN-10: 0983608806

Library of Congress control number: 2011931718

Suggested bibliographic citation for this publication:
Grayzel, John and others. *Human Security in an Insecure World*, ed. Michael Dravis.
 Transcript of an Interactive Dialogue sponsored by the Bahá'í Chair for World Peace at
 the University of Maryland. Falls Church, VA: Dialogue & Consultation Press, 2012.

Excerpts from the Interactive Dialogue are available online at:
http://www.youtube.com/user/BahaiPeaceChair
(select Playlist "Second Interactive Dialogue - Human Security")

For more information on the Bahá'í Chair for World Peace, visit:
http://www.bahaipeacechair.umd.edu

Book design by Peggy Weickert, University of Maryland, Design Services

This publication was made possible, in part, through the generosity of The Muhammed Ali Faizi Memorial Fund.

"…[T]he primary challenge in dealing with issues of peace is to raise the context to the level of principle, as distinct from pure pragmatism. For, in essence, peace stems from an inner state supported by a spiritual or moral attitude, and it is chiefly in evoking this attitude that the possibility of enduring solutions can be found."
　　　　 – Universal House of Justice, "The Promise of World Peace" (1985)

༄

"The 1994 'Human Development Report' by the United Nations Development Programme (UNDP) was the first to mention human security publicly in the international community. This report defined human security as providing safety for the people from hunger, diseases, oppression and other chronic threats as well as protecting them from sudden and hurtful disruptions in the pattern of daily life."
　　　　 – Ministry of Foreign Affairs of Japan, "The Trust Fund for
　　　　　　 Human Security: For the 'Human-centered' 21st Century" (2007)

༄

"To build a world in which the security of individuals is a priority, we must empower nation-states and demand that they provide both responsive governance internally and effective collaboration internationally. But if this state of affairs is to become the touchstone of global governance, the motivation for governments to conform will largely correspond to the motivations of their individual citizens and the commitment of those citizens to a shared set of clearly articulated foundational principles. Such principles would include not only security for themselves, but also the responsibility to be agents of security for others."
　　　　 – John Grayzel, "Human Security as a Foundational Principle
　　　　　　 of Global Governance" (2012)

CONTENTS

A NOTE ON D&C PRESS

This book inaugurates a new publishing enterprise—Dialogue & Consultation Press—launched by John Grayzel, the former holder of the Bahá'í Chair for World Peace at the University of Maryland. D&C Press defines "dialogue" as a sharing of thoughts and experiences that promotes a common understanding of the complexities of an issue, even if no agreement emerges on possible solutions. "Consultation" is a joint effort to produce a shared understanding on the nature of, and responses to, a problem of mutual concern.

The purpose of D&C Press is to publish dialogues and consulations of enduring value that feature discussants of capacity addressing major issues and actions related to peace. D&C titles illuminate the background circumstances, associated experiences, and thinking of key interlocutors in a format that intellectually engages readers.

A unique aspect of Dialogue & Consultation Press is that its publications are augmented by the inclusion of an original, annotated bibliography that provides a distillation of insightful perspectives relevant to the subject of the associated dialogue. Together with the dialogue, the bibliography seeks to provide a succinct but thoughtful introduction to the subject at hand.

In an increasingly interdependent world, the need for dialogue and consultation to manage the convergence of both distinct interests and diverse principles is one of the central challenges to achieving a world at peace. To help recognize this convergence and, hopefully, channel it into a cooperative and mutually beneficial effort is a primary purpose of Dialogue and Consultation Press.

Titles selected for inclusion in the D&C Press catalogue will be drawn, primarily, from three sources:

1) Dialogues sponsored by the Bahá'í Chair for World Peace;
2) Dialogues sponsored by others who share the goals of the press, including departments of the University of Maryland (UMD) and academic units and think tanks not affiliated with UMD;
3) Other significant dialogues relevant to building world peace that were: a) previously published but are now out of print; or b) never formally published.

FOREWORD

A core mission of the Bahá'í Chair for World Peace at the University of Maryland is to promote forums that enable the scholarly community and the wider public to go beyond the exchange of ideas to mutually exploring, in a consultative fashion, perspectives that challenge prevailing assumptions and established thinking on major issues of peace. For this reason, the second Bahá'í Chair for World Peace Interactive Dialogue—held at the University of Maryland on November 19, 2009 before an audience of professors, students, university administrators, and other guests—adhered to a concept of dialogue as a process that encourages a common quest for truth. Utilizing this approach, individuals offer their knowledge, thoughts, and beliefs while recognizing and incorporating those of their interlocutors in an exchange that leads to deeper understanding.

The theme of the second Interactive Dialogue was human security. Among the questions it posed were the following: What is human security and what are its purposes? What practical measures will advance human security? What role can "deep values, higher principles" play in achieving human security?

Over the last decade or so the concept of human security—which seeks to transcend the traditional doctrine of national security by protecting people against threats to their physical safety, economic wellbeing, and dignity as human beings—has received increasing attention from the highest levels of the UN, national and international diplomatic, development, and defense departments, the scholarly community, and from development and defense practitioners. While certainly not a panacea, the human security approach tries to recognize the complexities and interdependences we must grapple with in today's international environment.

I would like to express my profound gratitude to Patrick Cronin, Kishan Manocha, Mishkat al-Moumin, and Constance Newman for participating in the Interactive Dialogue. Much appreciation is due to Jan Tunney, Bengu Caliskan Selvi, and Barbara Zweig (of PlanIt Now LLC) for their invaluable efforts in planning and coordinating the myriad details required to hold an event like the Interactive Dialogue. Farinaz Firouzi stepped in at literally the last moment and guided the Dialogue event with distinction and skill to a successful conclusion.

I would also like to acknowledge Michael Dravis for editing the transcript, adding explanatory notes to it, and preparing the appendices and annotated bibliography.

John Grayzel,
Bahá'í Chair for World Peace (2006-2011)
University of Maryland, College Park, MD

INTRODUCTION

Human Security as a Foundational Principle of Global Governance:
Reflections on "Human Security in an Insecure World"

by
John Grayzel

The Dialogue presented in this book is guided by two methodologies available for wider application by individuals and communities wishing to enhance their understandings of, and responses to, current dynamics that are transforming the fragmented world community into an interdependent global society and, eventually, a global civilization.

One of those concepts is the Bahá'í model of group consultation. This concept centers on the idea that when a group convenes to discuss a shared concern, everyone—meaning not only particular individuals such as hosts, speakers, or experts but also audience members and listeners as well—should strive to move from the presentation of different ideas to mutual understanding and the formation of a consensus for action. Such a shared understanding and consensus, to be sure, must begin with the perspectives and experiences of *individuals*. However, through a process of consultation those individual contributions become the "bricks" of one edifice that all participants have helped construct and in which they all wish to reside.

The second methodology is called Bohmian dialogue. This term refers to the physicist David Bohm, who was a passionate advocate of the idea that dialogue should go beyond a mere exchange of ideas and instead serve as a mechanism through which each participant's mind transitions from an "old" to a "new" understanding. Whereas Bahá'í consultation focuses on the objective of achieving group consensus as a basis for action, in Bohmian dialogue the goal is less a consensus with others leading to specific action and more a transformation of each person's own thoughts and commitments.

As readers of the Dialogue in this publication will observe, the discussants are unique individuals whose diverse knowledge, action, and reflection greatly complement each other. Each of them possesses enormous real-world experience in addressing the challenges of achieving human security at the national and international levels. Dr. Patrick

Cronin has served in high-level positions at the U.S. National Defense University, the United States Agency for International Development (USAID), and many other key organizations. Dr. Kishan Manocha is a lawyer and a psychiatrist who has worked within the context of post-conflict situations, including war crimes tribunals in Africa. Dr. Mishkat al-Moumin, the first minister of the environment in the interim Iraqi government established after the U.S. intervention (and also the first woman to serve in that cabinet), draws heavily on her experiences as a bureaucrat who tried to manage an extremely challenging political and social environment. Finally, the Hon. Constance Newman—among many other roles—served as assistant secretary of state for African affairs and deputy administrator of USAID's Africa Bureau. She brings the perspective of an official who has regularly grappled with the reality that most problems of a seemingly political and technical nature actually stem from the dynamics of human relations. Drawing from this insight, Secretary Newman describes with clarity and feeling how international efforts to achieve common action ultimately depend on choices made by individuals and groups about whether or not they will work together effectively. She reminds us that, as individuals, we must take personal responsibility for the decisions we make; these often require a choice of either sacrificing our immediate interests or exacerbating dissatisfaction, insecurity, and even conflict within a larger group. In fact, a positive expression of this choice is reflected in the Dialogue itself: readers will note how the unique personal perspectives of each discussant unveil themselves in a rolling fashion in the course of the discussion and how the participants, by listening carefully to each other's ideas, seemingly converge in their thoughts and positions.

The discussants begin the Dialogue by sharing their experiences on the question of human security. Collectively, they agree that human security starts with an acknowledgment that each of us has our own security needs as people. They highlight how the concept of human security emerged as a paradigm after the end of the Cold War, when the old "political-security" justification for development spending was increasingly challenged. They note that a key moment in the emergence of human security came in 1994, when the United Nations Development Programme defined and explored the concept in its groundbreaking publication entitled *Human Development Report*. Then, as part of their initial explanations, panel members stress the classic elements that constitute peoples' basic needs: housing, food, water, physical protection, and community stability. All of these are standard human security elements that feature prominently in most definitions of the doctrine. The panel then discusses how the doctrine of human security influences international behavior today.

The Dialogue participants recognize that the United States Government has not adopted "human security" as an official development doctrine. Nevertheless, official U.S. development programs focus on many issues that fall under the human security rubric, especially programs that are implemented in what are called "fragile" or "failed" states. The panel then coalesces around the observation that other countries often perceive the United States' search for national security as a cause of insecurity. Examples include U.S. military interventions in Iraq and Afghanistan and also U.S. policy interventions such as "the war on drugs" or "free trade." Actions such as these are designed to protect American security interests, but often they directly or indirectly damage people and institutions in other countries. Damaging another country while pursuing one's own security is not unique to the U.S— rather, it is at the core of the reality called "war." Yet at this moment in history, United States actions of this kind are possibly more frequent and prominent than any other nation because the U.S., in general, holds such a preponderance of power within the international system and projects that power worldwide in its "global war on terror."

The panel's observations, however, do not indicate support for what would be a classic proposal to limit engagement in the affairs of other nations. Rather, what emerges from their commentaries is a sketch of a world characterized by increasing interdependence. Developing this sketch further, the panel converges on the fact that the world's need for human security cannot be addressed by any particular nation working alone; nor do they believe bilateral initiatives are adequate to meet the challenges of today. Rather, the problems and solutions of the contemporary world, if they are to be addressed effectively in a sustainable fashion, increasingly require global actions that are undertaken in a sustained, systematic, and multilateral fashion.

However, cross-national, and thus inherently cross-cultural, actions almost inevitably engender increased complexity. To better harmonize such efforts, multilateral human security initiatives require more than better-coordinated operations and policies. Among the needed additions to achieve sustained common action on global issues is the establishment of shared motivations. In turn, such motivations require the existence of compatible values such as the acceptance of common global principles about human security itself. This issue—the need for a new global ethic—goes beyond what has been the focus of classic diplomacy with its emphasis on state sovereignty and reconciling divergent interests through negotiations. Diplomacy's focus on national interests emerged from common foundational principles established in the wake of the Peace of Westphalia of 1648 and the resulting restructuring of the international order. Diplomatic negotiations that adhere to "Westphalia principles" almost always avoid delving into what are perceived to be quagmires of underlying principles that relate to deeper social, cultural, ideological or spiritual values. In short, the Westphalia approach relegates key issues to the internal prerogatives of each state rather than allowing them to be matters of common concern to the community of states.

As panel members seemingly adjust their personal views to each other's perspectives, one sees how they look again at their own experiences and, based on reflecting anew on those experiences, together begin to refocus their discussion on how a series of emerging global principles are either being accepted or rejected around the world based largely on prevailing local conditions. Thus, although the goal sought may be global in significance, reflecting on history highlights the reality that a rising global principle concerning human security seems to emerge from changes in the experiences of individuals and groups within their local environment. An example of this phenomenon is the record of both national and international responses to HIV/AIDS. Over the years, and across countries and circumstances, it has been repeatedly observed that individuals support proactive, positive responses to HIV/AIDS only after they witness the effects of the pandemic on someone they personally know or when their own interests—such as business owners who must deal with absenteeism by ill employees—begin to suffer due to the direct or indirect consequences of the disease.

Building on recognition of this reality—what can be called the "individuality of large-group response"—the panel in various ways highlights how many of the changes that are occurring globally are closely tied to the rapidly increasing connectivity among people empowered by new communications technologies such as Twitter, Facebook, cell phones, and text messaging. These technologies have vastly increased the ways, means, and extent to which people can share their experiences with others locally, nationally, and globally. A world of possibilities is now only beginning to emerge in terms of new ways of forming local, global, and "glocal" (global-local) support networks around particular grassroots and international situations and interests. In terms of connectivity, the panel highlights the dynamic that is developing between larger phenomena (i.e., global) and their smaller expression (i.e., local). This trend is prodding international security policy away from its traditional focus on the security of nation-states in favor of an approach that emphasizes the security of individuals and communities *within* and *across* states. In essence, this is the core of the new human security doctrine. Most critically, the panel discussion highlights how individuals themselves, in connecting with others, are playing a critical role in advancing the doctrine of human security on the global level.

A particularly dramatic example of what individuals can achieve is brought forth when the panel discusses the 1994 Rwandan genocide and the part played in the cataclysm by Roméo Dallaire, the Canadian general who led the United Nations peacekeeping force deployed in that country. Dallaire and his troops attempted to protect threatened Rwandans in ways consonant with the doctrine of human security, but their actions failed because they were not supported by the UN headquarters or by key UN members such as the U.S. and Belgium (Rwanda' former colonial power). The discussion of General Dallaire brings the panel to consider the proposition that if we want to change the way nations act, it is we ourselves—as individuals—who must change the way nations understand and express the principles of human security. This insight touches on the core of how we see ourselves as humans and as members of families and communities; it also brings to the forefront the need to recognize those personal understandings and beliefs that can motivate us to become advocates of new global foundational principles in response to changing world conditions.

During the Dialogue, the spirit of Bohmian dialogue and Bahá'í consultation prevails as the participants increasingly seem to develop a shared introspection based on their own lives and thoughts. What they propose are not just expressions of their preconceived propositions. In fact, many of their individual responses significantly diverge from what one might typically expect from them based on their established perspectives. Kishan Manocha (the psychiatrist), for example, emerges as the strongest proponent of meaningful action as an alternative to endless individual self-analysis. Constance Newman, the experienced bureaucrat and administrator, drills down to the fundamental truth that our views of the world are often inextricably tied to our family life, especially the nurturing we receive as children from our parents. This affects not only how we act, but also how we raise the next generation and how we see ourselves as part of a larger, inter-generational process. Patrick Cronin, a recognized expert in policy analysis, suggests that we go beyond simply weighing immediate empirical factors and urges us to examine the implications of historical experience and the deeper values that provide enduring motivations for peoples and societies. Mishkat al-Moumin, the former government minister, champions the concerns of people at the grassroots level; she argues that effective governance begins and ends with consideration of the direct effects of policies on the daily lives of people.

After reflecting on the thoughts of the panel, among the many provocative ideas that emerge is the following proposition: *if we hope to build a world in which the security of individuals is a priority, then we must empower nation-states and demand that they provide both responsive governance internally and effective collaboration internationally.* But if this state of affairs is to become the touchstone of global governance, the motivation for governments to conform will largely correspond to the motivations of their individual citizens and the commitment of those citizens to a shared set of clearly articulated foundational principles. Such principles would include not only security for themselves, but also the responsibility to be agents of security for others and personal responsibility to take immediate action in their particular circumstances to make this happen.[1]

---

[1] Further analysis of the need and status of emerging foundational principles can be found on the website "Foundational Principles of Global Governance Monitor" (www.foundationalprinciplesmonitor.com). In addition, see the website "Crossroads of Peace" (www.crossroadsofpeace.org); under the link for Dialogues and Consultations, view videos addressing human security and related matters, including Bohmian dialogue and the Bahá'í concept of consultation.

Eventually, the Dialogue participants return to the initial question: why has the doctrine of human security not received official support from the world's major powers, most especially the United States? Here, in my view, the discussion becomes an example of transformative dialogue that leads to new understandings.

Looking back at the Dialogue, we see that it begins with an outline of the need for, and potentials of, human security that fully supports its worthiness as a new policy response to international realities. Subsequently, panelists surveyed some of the major hurdles to implementing human security as a policy. What becomes apparent is that few people or nations—and certainly not the United States— seem to oppose a doctrine under which people enjoy broader security in their lives. Moreover, few countries—and certainly not the United States—seem to question the proposition that "security" issues are not just pragmatic in nature but also encompass fundamental human rights. In the case of the United States, many of these rights are traceable to, or articulated in, foundational documents such as the (American) Declaration of Independence and the (U.S.-inspired and sponsored) Universal Declaration of Human Rights.

In this light, the challenge of human security seems at first to reside in overcoming the limitations of realpolitik and what one nation or group of nations can do to advance the doctrine in the face of international norms ensconced under the Westphalian theory and practice of state sovereignty. Upon further consideration, however, one can see that over the past several decades, these principles of sovereignty have been repeatedly ignored during interventions undertaken by the United States, other major powers, and the United Nations—against, or at least without the approval, of the governments whose sovereignty is being violated (i.e., Sudan, Burma, Bosnia/Kosovo, Timor, South Africa, Sierra Leone, Liberia, Libya, etc.). Some of these cases represent direct military interventions, others less direct means such as politically determined economic sanctions. However, all of these interventions faced the challenge of formidable obstacles to enforcing compliance with human security norms, but this reality did not stop the attempt to do so; and in many instances, significant successes were achieved.

It is precisely here, at the crossroads of pragmatics and principles, where the Dialogue raises new perspectives on the reluctance of many nations to accept human security as a foundational principle. As previously noted, Dialogue participants forged a consensus that, in the final analysis, human security will prevail only when it is understood as more than a pragmatic policy but also as a foundational principle that each of us, as an individual, upholds. From this perspective, I believe that four powerful and critical realizations arise that represent major contributions of the Dialogue to prevailing understandings of human security and its acceptance in theory and practice.

First is the proposition that a major impediment to the acceptance of human security is not the operational policies required to enforce the doctrine. Rather, it is that many governments do not want their foreign policies to be "dictated" by commonly accepted principles. This was dramatically demonstrated in the case of the Rwandan genocide (discussed above), when the governments of the United States and Belgium both repeatedly avoided using the word "genocide" to describe what was happening in that country. In that case, the U.S. and Belgium both feared the possibly negative domestic political consequences of intervening in a messy internal conflict; similarly, both countries sought to avoid having to act in accordance with international obligations triggered by the UN genocide convention.[2] Thus, what may hamper acceptance of human security as a foundational principle for international action is not the propositions of the principle itself, but rather the fear that if it becomes a global foundational principle it will further limit a state's authority to act—or not act—based on calculations of national interest.

Second, the panel shared its realization that the sustainability of *national* foundational principles often rests on the existence and strength of corresponding *individual* foundational principles; the latter, in fact, are often the enablers of the former. Thus, one can interpret Japan's emergence as a champion of human security as partially a reflection of traditional Japanese principles of shared social responsibility. Those principles stand in contrast, for example, to the American ethos of individualism. Different, but likewise deeply held, social and cultural orientations in favor of individual responsibility for group security are found in Scandinavian countries and also in Canada.

---

[2] See Holly J. Burkhalter, "The Question of Genocide: The Clinton Administration and Rwanda," *World Policy Journal* 11 (Winter, 1994/1995): 44-54.

Not coincidentally, those countries are strong advocates of human security as an international principle.[3]

Third, the Dialogue on human security highlights the need for greatly expanded dialogues on human security, not only among "experts" but also among the general citizenry of the world. These must be dialogues leading to an awareness that it is each individual's own principles that help form and sustain their nation's principles. In other words, each individual's commitment to human security as a foundational principle is a prerequisite to advancing the larger foundational principles of human security. Under such a process, not only does human security become a principle of global governance but the proposition that pragmatic action should occur within the context of agreed upon principles also becomes a principle of global governance.

Fourth and finally, it should be noted that this understanding of the vital role of individuals and their own foundational principles in establishing larger social and global principles is a converse of the more commonly held assumption that society forms the person rather than the person forms society. As such, it is not only a powerful insight into the origins and status of larger foundational principles, but also a demonstration of the power of dialogue to go beyond an exchange of ideas to become an impetus for deeper consultation as a prelude to action. In this regard, the Dialogue on human security also demonstrated the value of participation by diverse parties—in this case, audience members through their questions and comments. This last observation argues for the establishment of more open and continuous forms of dialogues and consultations as the basis of addressing issues of global concern in general and, specifically, for establishing the doctrine of human security as a foundation of global governance.[4]

---

[3] The Canadian Human Rights Commission cites "the thinking of Irwin Cotler (Canadian Minister of Justice) on this matter, especially his view that the foundational principle in all matters of national security and human rights is to find their meeting ground in a conception of 'human security.'" See the Canadian Human Rights Commissions website at [www.chrc-ccdp.ca/research_program_recherche/ns_sn/page12-eng.aspx] (accessed 18 June 2011). See also Irwin Cotler, "Thinking Outside the Box: Foundational Principles for a Counter-Terrorism Law and Policy," in *The Security of Freedom: Essays on Canada's Anti-Terrorism Bill,* eds. Ronald J. Daniels et al. (Toronto: University of Toronto Press, 2001), p. 112.

[4] The website "Crossroads of Peace" (see note 1) and the new publishing concern called Dialogue and Consultations Press, LLC, have been established to advance the process of dialogue as practiced under the Bohmian model and the Bahá'í concept of consultation.

INTERACTIVE DIALOGUE TRANSCRIPT

Editor's note: The following is based on an audio recording of the event. The transcript has been edited for clarity, including some revision of words and phrases; select explanatory footnotes have been appended.

Interactive Dialogue Participants
(Biographies of the participants can be found in Appendix 1)

> Patrick Cronin
> Kishan Manocha
> Mishkat al-Moumin
> Constance Newman
> John Grayzel, *Moderator*

Introduction

J. GRAYZEL: During the first Baha'i Chair for World Peace Interactive Dialogue, entitled "The Humanity of Diplomacy,"[5] the panel's conclusion was that, in the end, diplomacy really is a matter of people-to-people and heart-to-heart contacts. But the question is, how does one go beyond that perspective? We are, today, constantly bombarded by the word "security." In the face of this, the questions we must ask are: "How well do we understand security?" and "How well do we understand what's needed for it?" These are the themes I hope we can explore today. I'm hoping

We are, today, constantly bombarded by the word "security." In the face of this, the questions we must ask are: "How well do we understand security?" and "How well do we understand what's needed for it?"

---

[5] Viewable online at [http://www.youtube.com/watch?v=G2cUsDmIwUw]; accessed 11 January 2012. The proceedings of the first Interactive Dialogue are also available in published form (purchasable from Amazon.com): John Grayzel and others, *The Humanity of Diplomacy: People and Diplomacy in the 21st Century* (Charleston, SC: BookSurge, 2009). Video of this, the second Interactive Dialogue, is available at [http://www.youtube.com/user/BahaiPeaceChair], select Playlist "Second Interactive Dialogue - Human Security"; accessed 11 January 2012.

that the four of you [the panelists], in exchanging ideas, will broaden the discussion that I find is very much compartmentalized among different groups. One compartmentalization arises between those who have a classic view of security that is built on the concept of nation-state security, which we've had since the Peace of Westphalia,[6] and a newer concept called "human security," which is very broad.

To get a sense of human security as a concept, I would like to begin with Constance Newman, who has had an enormous range of experiences. Connie, you've been everywhere from the inner circle of the U.S. government to the people on the ground in refugee camps. I wonder if you would begin our discussion by sharing with us

---

[6] The Peace of Westphalia (1648)—often called, although less properly so, the *Treaty* of Westphalia—is the collective name given to the series of diplomatic agreements ending the Thirty Years' War (1618-1648), a cycle of conflicts that raged among various European powers and that visited tremendous death and destruction, principally in regions of Germany (then a geographical area, not a unified political unit).

The Peace of Westphalia is considered a watershed because it ushered in a new era of international affairs. Former U.S. Secretary of State Henry Kissinger has summarized the significance of Westphalia in these terms: "Out of this carnage [of the Thirty Years' War] emerged the modern state system as defined by the Treaty of Westphalia of 1648, the basic principles of which have shaped international relations to this day. The treaty's foundation was the doctrine of sovereignty, which declared a state's domestic conduct and institutions to be beyond the reach of other states." See Kissinger, *Does America Need a Foreign Policy?* (New York: Simon and Schuster, 2001), 21.

The significance of Westphalia as the origin and symbol of an enduring international order is revealed in the following passage: "On one occasion in 1940 Hitler was supposed to have said that he would impose his victorious peace treaty at Munster in Westphalia, thus putting an end to the European state system that had been established there in 1648." See John Lukacs, *The Hitler of History* (New York: Alfred A. Knopf, 1997), 247 note *.

A comprehensive study of the Thirty Years' War, including the peace process conducted at Westphalia, can be found in Peter H. Wilson, *The Thirty Years War: Europe's Tragedy* (Cambridge, MA: Harvard University Press, 2009).

your observations on what you see as the different spectrums of understanding that people have in terms of security?

Three Approaches to Human Security

C. NEWMAN: What I want to do is take the question from the point of view of nations. My answer first of all is, "It depends." A nation's understanding of security depends on the extent to which there is security and stability in the nation. It depends on the extent to which the people are involved in governance—I'm not saying democracy, just the extent to which they are involved. It depends on the leadership and how ethical it is. What I want to do is take three different countries and describe security in the short time that I have.

First of all, there are countries that get it and do it. There are countries that get it, but don't do it. And there are countries that don't have a clue. In the first group, I put Botswana. Botswana has security; it has democracy; it has the highest growth rate of African countries, and it has the second highest HIV/AIDS rate. The leadership there has decided to allocate resources and to talk about it and to bring about change. And they've integrated human security into their whole approach to security of the nation.

Ethiopia, on the other hand, gets it but doesn't do it. Ethiopia has put a great deal of money into education and health on the one hand, but at the same time, there are all these complaints about the government's human rights violations, particularly

There are countries that get [human security], but don't do it. And there are countries that don't have a clue. In the first group, I put Botswana.

3

in the Somalia region.[7] So Ethiopia gets it, but it doesn't do it when it's not in the government's interest.

The third country is the Democratic Republic of the Congo, and it doesn't have a clue, in part because it's still very much coming out of conflict. It really isn't out of conflict yet. It's still experiencing conflict in the east.[8] The leadership there has not had the time, the interest, or the resources to deal with human security and doesn't even try to talk about it.

J. GRAYZEL: Dr. Patrick Cronin has had a very distinguished and varied career. One of those careers was as head of the Bureau of Policy and Program Coordination for USAID, and I had the honor of serving under him. At that time, I couldn't help seeing, over and over again, that he, in many ways, was trying to tell people in our government that they weren't getting it.

Connie Newman has stated that the governance of a country very much determines whether people in the country really experience *human* security and not just what the government

---

[7] A January 2009 report by Human Rights Watch states: "The Ethiopian government's human rights record remains poor, marked by an ever-hardening intolerance towards meaningful political dissent or independent criticism. Ethiopian military forces have continued to commit war crimes and other serious abuses with impunity in the course of counterinsurgency campaigns in Ethiopia's eastern Somali Region and in neighboring Somalia." See "Ethiopia: Country Summary" (available from [http://www.hrw.org/en/node/79222]; accessed 1 March 2010).

[8] A report by the Center for American Progress concludes: "For 13 years, the people of eastern Congo have been ensnared in a tangled web of armed groups—from foreign rebels to the Congo's own army—who prey on Congolese civilians and, with collaboration from governments and multinational corporations, strip the country of its immense natural wealth." See John Prendergast and Noel Atama, "Eastern Congo: An Action Plan to End the World's Deadliest War," 16 July 2009 (available from [http://www.enoughproject.org/publications/eastern-congo-action-plan-end-worlds-deadliest-war]; accessed 16 March 2010).

defines as *national* security. But, within that broader understanding, when I look at our own government, I sometimes wonder, do *we* get it? I know that this concept of human security has been around since the early 1990s, but the U.S. government hasn't seemed to be willing to engage it in a major fashion. Maybe I'm being unfair. So, I would like your reflection about where in our government human security strikes a note, or doesn't strike a note, and what might be done to move us ahead on this idea?

Does the U.S. "Get" Human Security?

P. CRONIN: Let me just take a bite of the apple, because it's a big topic and we can't really do justice to it. I recall fondly the days back in USAID when you were very much trying to educate me on the complexity of global security challenges and I was very sympathetic. But at the same time, how could we take that construct of human security and implement it into something that people can do practically? How can you take another step forward and actually do something amid complexity? It's a topic that I'm still grappling with and it's one that I've put together in a new book called *Global Strategic Assessment 2009*,[9] which looks at 125 broad issues and tries to bring them together.

Unfortunately, at the end of the day, there is no simple, unifying concept for policy implementation. There may be unifying principles that we can rely on, however. So, does the United States government "get it?"; does it define what "it" is here and talk about whether or not it even has a moral compass when it is trying to determine

...how could we take that construct of human security and implement it into something that people can do practically? How can you take another step forward and actually do something amid complexity?

---

[9] Patrick Cronin, ed., *Global Strategic Assessment 2009: America's Security Role in a Changing World* (Washington, DC: National Defense University Press, 2009).

policy? How do we do that, given our secular government structure? How do we do it when we are a reductionist society, meaning that we are in the habit of reducing complex problems into finite issues so that we can solve them, fix them, go in and turn them over to someone else? Rather than seeing the continuum, rather than seeing the connections and the connectivity, we deliberately try to parse it into sound bites and tweets.

Security Challenges in the Twenty-first Century

Looking to the world we're heading into over the next couple of decades, I'd like to identify some of the challenges we face economically, politically, and in terms of the dissemination of information—which challenges state authority in that individuals now have as much information as many states. We need to think about the impact of energy and the environment and how they are now becoming security factors—they're no longer just important issues, they actually threaten our security in this century. We need to think about fragile states, states that don't deliver on security, social goods, or economic opportunity, and become a security risk abroad, not just to the people in the country itself.

We need to think about violent extremism, which is often really a transnational movement. There are situations in which violent, local extremists are infected by a foreign ideology, and this ideology becomes refracted through local dynamics and you have something new—something we haven't dealt with. It's not just national; it's not even just a non-state actor within a state. There are global connections, but it's not global terrorism. It's something more complex than that.

Then we have issues of dealing with the changing nature of conflict itself. One of the things we've learned as a government— this is where you could say there's been some

We need to think about fragile states, states that don't deliver on security, social goods, or economic opportunity, and become a security risk abroad, not just to the people in the country itself.

6

incremental learning—is the whole concept of counterinsurgency theory, that whole renaissance in counterinsurgency. Why do I think that's a slight improvement? It's a step backwards, you could say. No, it's war, but it's a concept looking forward because it's become a focus on *people*—populations—understanding that it's not about killing adversaries, it's about protecting people. To protect people, it's not simply a military means, it's something that's mostly non-military. But there's a military component as well. That's an old concept. It's not a new concept.

I studied in the United Kingdom and I was taught by two great men, one a great British military historian, Sir Michael Howard, who set up the War Studies program at Kings College London in the 1950s. He did this in direct response to the United States military history approach, where we turned everything into military operations. We still do that as a government. So, when Connie Newman was trying to make sense out of human security in Africa, it struck a chord. Even before we had an AFRICOM,[10] we had a military that wanted to make a campaign plan out of whatever crisis that would occur in that continent. When she was in government, Connie had to figure out

---

[10] AFRICOM is the acronym for Africa Command, the division of the U.S. Department of Defense responsible for operations in that region of the world. According to its official mission statement, "United States Africa Command, in concert with other U.S. Government agencies and international partners, conducts sustained security engagement through military-to-military programs, military-sponsored activities, and other military operations as directed to promote a stable and secure African environment in support of U.S. foreign policy."

AFRICOM has been the subject of controversy originating both within the United States and across Africa. Among other criticisms, opponents of AFRICOM charge that it contributes to a dangerous pattern whereby U.S. foreign policy has been unduly militarized. Despite ongoing efforts, AFRICOM has been unable to establish a headquarters on the continent in the face of nearly unanimous opposition by the governments of Africa.

how to bring the policy instruments of economic development, humanitarian assistance, and mix them with diplomacy and other means to try to stabilize countries, advance prosperity, build institutions and, ultimately, build human security.

Building human security is a great challenge. We're learning that. Then, of course, there's the bigger problem of the proliferation of weapons of mass destruction that could threaten whole populations with extinction. It's not just the nuclear issue that we're so caught up with today. My wife is in Dubai right now with Graham Allison[11] and a small group at the World Economic Forum looking at terrorism and weapons of mass destruction, especially nuclear weapons. One can be scared by a lot of scenarios that are unlikely, but because they would have a high impact, they need to be prevented.

But one worries about the life sciences and developments in that field, because it's not the people in this room with the moral compass who are going to be the perpetrators of this. There will be, unfortunately, disaffected individuals who can now do something completely out of sight of satellites—squirrels in a basement, if you will. And they can spread biological agents in a way that could be a big problem.

How do we organize against that? How do we reconcile human security—with the understanding we're trying to protect humans—and how do we bring our humanity into policy and yet still organize in our communities, mostly states as Connie was talking about, but not just states? The Obama administration is trying to build a global

How do we reconcile human security—with the understanding we're trying to protect humans— and how do we bring our humanity into policy and yet still organize in our communities…?

---

[11] Graham Allison, a prominent political scientist and Harvard University professor who is best known, perhaps, for his seminal study *Essence of Decision: Explaining the Cuban Missile Crisis* (first published in 1971).

architecture of engagement that doesn't just deal with state-to-state issues.

So, in the diplomatic realm President Obama doesn't just speak with Hu Jintao,[12] he also tries to speak to the people of China directly. But as we've seen, China doesn't quite allow that to happen as freely as it can happen at the University of Maryland in College Park. So, the world is both working on this global-transnational set of trends in human security and it's also still very much mired in nineteenth century, balance-of-power politics. Both are co-existing. The American government is only adapting part way. It sort of gets the problem, but it doesn't know how to move forward.

J. GRAYZEL: Connie [Newman], would you mind if I challenge you a little on something you said? The group of states you identified—and I think you gave good examples—the group of states that get it and act, that get it and don't act, and that don't get it at all. The doctrine of human security as it's promulgated by the Canadians and Japanese seems to say to us that we have to focus more on individuals and care more about them.

One of the questions I have, and I guess I'll refer to my own experience, is that in some of those countries you named, I would say, there is a government in place. But when you talk about the Congo, where I served, is there really a government, or do we fool ourselves that there is a government? Do we not have to look behind the government and say who are the people and how can we get to the people and see whether they get it and how we can help them?

...the world is both working on this global-transnational set of trends in human security and it's also still very much mired in nineteenth century, balance-of-power politics.

---

[12] President of the People's Republic of China and General Secretary of the Communist Party of China.

U.S. Insecurity Hinders Human Security Worldwide

C. NEWMAN: Yes, but remember I said at first that there are the principles of a stable, secure, governance with the peoples' involvement. The peoples' involvement is extremely important and I wanted just to say to Patrick [Cronin] that I think that one reason that the United States has not really taken human security as seriously as it should is the feeling of insecurity in this country. We talk a lot about security, and we spend a lot of money because we feel insecure. Botswana feels secure. I think that we ought to spend some time today trying to figure out why the United States has not taken the position of a Canada or a Japan with respect to human security. Why is it that we don't even want to use the language of human security? We started to use this kind of language in the Bush national strategy paper,[13] but using the language is not enough. There has to be resources to back up the language. There has to be action behind the language. I just think it will be something very interesting for us to explore in this dialogue.

J. GRAYZEL: I couldn't agree with you more, and I would almost want to say, "So, why not?" We'll get back to the "why not" because I think that is the key question. The answer is also a challenge to everyone out here and all of us as Americans. We have Dr. Mishkat al-Moumin, who was the first environmental minister in the interim government of Iraq. We talk among ourselves as Americans.

...I think that one reason that the United States has not really taken human security as seriously as it should is the feeling of insecurity in this country. We talk a lot about security, and we spend a lot of money because we feel insecure.

---

[13] As mandated by law, annually the executive branch of the United States Government must present the U.S. Congress with a "national security strategy report." Two such reports—both entitled *The National Security Strategy of the United States of America*—were issued in President George W. Bush's name, the first in September 2002 and the second in March 2006.

We are in the United States. We are Americans and we should probably begin with "doctor heal thyself," but we should also listen to other people.

Now you've been on the other side. You're one of the people who has moved back and forth between roles. Please address the theme we're talking about—human security—and what we have to do from a non-American perspective. How do the people of Iraq see it, feel it, even understand it? What word do they even use for it? Or are we living in our own bubble and unless we get out of it, we're never going to be able to adequately address the question that was raised?

Basic Services or Democracy First?

M. AL-MOUMIN: I think to stabilize post-conflict nations to prevent insurgency and address them if they occur—and Iraq is not an exception in this case—you need to provide basic environmental needs. The first thing that needs to be done in a post-conflict situation is provide safe drinking water, provide sanitation services, provide electricity and trash pickup. If these four things are not provided, you are going to face political instability and even insurgency.

In Iraq, the insurgency that emerged provided these basic services. When I went to Sadr City in Baghdad, I had to step in sewer water up to my knees. And I met with a woman. She's illiterate, she doesn't speak English. She doesn't have a Ph.D. She looked at me and said, "Why can't they"— meaning the government—"provide safe drinking water? Why can't they come and pick up the trash, rather than shooting at us?" That woman was trying to drink from the sewer water because that was the only source of water available.

The first thing that needs to be done in a post-conflict situation is provide safe drinking water, provide sanitation services, provide electricity and trash pickup. If these four things are not provided, you are going to face political instability and even insurgency.

I felt I could not bear to talk about democracy and elections to that woman. By the end of the day, this woman went to the polls and voted for the radical leader, Muqtada al-Sadr,[14] because he provided basic services. He provided electricity, gasoline, water—you name it. The same thing is done by other insurgencies.

Human security is about meeting basic needs. If you don't meet them, you are going to face political instability and insurgency. It will continue to occur until you address these issues.

J. GRAYZEL: Can I go back? Do you think we got it? Or why didn't we get it? From the perspective of somebody in Iraq, why do you think we didn't get it?

Security is More Than Military Force

M. AL-MOUMIN: I think security is being understood, practiced, and interpreted as the mere use of force. Give me policemen! Give me military forces! Guns. Rockets. You name it. However, when you try to address or bring that up, wait a minute, there are basic needs here that must be met, the answer is "No, no, no, no. Let's provide security first. Let the troops work on security and *then* we'll provide other services."

I was in a cabinet meeting with Dr. Ayad Allawi, he was the prime minister at that time. He has a diploma in environment and environmental studies. The situation was so tense, the conversation was tense, between him and his

Human security is about meeting basic needs. If you don't meet them, you are going to face political instability and insurgency.

---

[14] An Iraqi Shiite leader, al-Sadr heads a militia known as the Mahdi Army. He enjoys a strong base of support in the poor Shiite neighborhoods of Baghdad and has been a vehement opponent of the U.S. presence in Iraq.

minister of the interior. The conversation was all about more guns, more weapons, more police forces, more army troops. I interrupted him a little bit by asking one question, "Do you think people will cooperate with your security plan if they go home and they open up the tap and there is no water?"

No insurgency can operate successfully without supporters among the people. That's impossible. So we talk a lot about foreign fighters in Iraq. That's right, they are a problem. However, there is local support for the insurgency because they provide services.

J. GRAYZEL: Dr. [Kishan] Manocha, I'd like to ask you for a reflection. The reason I'm turning to you is that I think you have engaged in a whole range of experiences, and among the things you've done is that you're a barrister, and the law tends to project that things are logical, that they fit in. You've also worked on human rights atrocities in Africa, which were about as opposite to what is rational as you can get. But in your experience, before we go further into what Connie [Newman] posed, I'd like to ask if you could reflect on this: Is there, in your experience, still another missing element?

I'll give you an example of what I mean because there was something specifically that brought this up just recently. There was just a broadcast on National Public Radio about the situation in Mongolia, which is a country I worked in for USAID. In the early 1990s, when the Soviet Union collapsed, Mongolia was in crisis because it depended on the Soviet Union for subsidies. It couldn't afford the fuel to heat its capital city [Ulan Bator], so half its population had to evacuate to the countryside to survive.

Today Mongolia has gigantic office buildings, millionaires, gold companies, but the thrust of the

The conversation was all about more guns, more weapons, more police forces, more army troops. I interrupted [the Prime Minister] a little bit by asking one question, "Do you think people will cooperate with your security plan if they go home and they open up the tap and there is no water?"

NPR story was how young Mongolians can no longer afford to help support their elderly parents. What would seem like economic progress, technical progress, has actually not translated into greater capacities, but seems to have translated into lesser capacities.

So, my question is, "Is there something else missing?" I think one of the reasons I ask this is because you're from England and the example I always use with my class is Sherlock Holmes and "The Hound of the Baskervilles." In that tale, the secret to solving the case was that the dogs didn't bark, which meant that they knew the murderer. So, is there something we're not picking up that you, in your experience, have also seen?

Spirituality, the "Missing Dimension" of Human Security

K. MANOCHA: Yes, there very much is. There's been a lot of discussion in the UK in the last year or two about the United Kingdom being a broken society. So, clearly, those who believe that and express that view are speaking to a reality implying that as a society, despite however advanced we are, at peace, with most of our basic needs being met in most places, there's something lacking. It's not entirely secure. In terms of the construction of the building of the country, it's as if the bricks and mortar are not quite in place.

I think it's because what we're lacking is the ability or vision of a full measure of human security, if you like. Material resources only take us so far. It doesn't complete the entire journey. That which is required to complete the journey and make our experience full is what most people intuitively are aware of. The vast majority of the world's population is intuitively aware of another dimension to their lives, which is a transcendental or spiritual part. It's that which defines their reality, defines their experience, shapes their experiences, shapes their relationships to others. It's those universal spiritual values—those transcendental values—that are the glue that holds society and us together.

So, yes, you can live in the most advanced technological society, but if there isn't deep compassion; there isn't fellow feeling; there isn't true empathy; there isn't the capacity to transcend our self-interest, then you will look at your neighbor and perhaps not feel what you need to feel to ensure that that person is secure, that person is being considered, that person's reality is being addressed. So this leads, ultimately, to a question of what is the source of those values? How can we inculcate, nurture those values and capacities in society, in individuals, amongst people over time and then, how can we then build the structures that can channel those qualities and values into meaningful service within society?

One of the things that has been coming out of some of these discussions in the UK in recent years is that what is really lacking—what is really missing is not just the values—but in acting on them in meaningful acts of service to society. So you're reminded of your neighbors; you're reminded of your family; you're reminded of your friends; and you're reminded of those others, those strangers who you don't know, but whose needs are your needs and you will respond to and address them. So I think that's where we're heading in this discussion of the missing dimension of our experience.

J. GRAYZEL: I want to add something as a qualifier. I may make the mistake of using different titles when addressing our discussants because I know some of these people in different settings and it's really interesting how titles change. In USAID, where Patrick [Cronin] was my boss, everybody goes by their first name. That was not a sign of disrespect. There was respect, and even the head of USAID you called by his first name. I think it reflected a deep personal relationship that people actually had to their work, seeing their organization as a community and not just a bureaucracy.

But you talked before about the complexities of what we can and can't handle, realistically. Can we handle, in our political structure, in our concepts, in our diplomacy, elements that Dr. Manocha just mentioned—elements that have to do with peoples' deeper beliefs and feelings? If not, what do we do about that if it's really the key to peoples' motivations?

Cosmopolitanism as a Response to Sovereignty

P. CRONIN: I wouldn't be overly pessimistic, but wouldn't say we're handling it particularly well. Going back to graduate school in the early 1980s in Oxford, there were two concepts that really had very little traction at the time. I remember that in our weekly seminars with Hedley Bull,[15] the concept of cosmopolitanism was much discussed. Cosmopolitanism is the idea that we are creating a global governance culture amongst elites— this cosmopolitan culture transcends national boundaries, transcends the more traditional concept of sovereignty, which is mostly supported still by our governments today.[16]

Cosmopolitanism is the idea that we are creating a global governance culture amongst elites— this cosmopolitan culture transcends national boundaries, transcends the more traditional concept of sovereignty, which is mostly supported still by our governments today.

---

[15] A prominent scholar of international relations (lived 1932-1985), his best-known work is entitled *The Anarchical Society* (first published in 1977).

[16] For discussion of the origin and evolution of the concept of cosmopolitanism, see Samuel Moyn, *The Last Utopia: Human Rights in History* (Cambridge, MA: Harvard University Press, 2010), 13-16, 20, 41.

Where my wife is today at the World Economic Forum is, in a sense, part of that cosmopolitan culture. But cosmopolitanism is also quite divorced from a lot of human security. What can cosmopolitanism do for, say, child soldiers rescued from the Lords Resistance Army in Uganda who are trying to be reintegrated back into rural society? That's a very different part of the human security dimension. That's how complex it is.

Piracy and the Need for Global Governance

The other concept that had no traction back many years ago was piracy, which we laughed at. Back then, we all thought, "Piracy is not going to be a big issue."

What cosmopolitanism and piracy both have in common today is that we see that these forces that transcend national boundaries, either sub-state actors, transnational actors, or global actors, and global consciousness, are increasingly important in our world today. Actually, state sovereignty hasn't withered away, but it is increasingly challenged to deal with both traditional concepts of security— and Connie [Newman] is right to say we're still very insecure despite the fact that we invest so much in security. But now we also are not prepared to deal with the adaptation at a human level, at a community, and a state level to build the architecture for global governance, what a lot of people call the "global commons," for instance.

We live in a globalized society; we're very dependent on the Internet, for example. Well, that's a cyber-domain that we are dependent on. We depend on maritime routes for our trade. Who provides the public good of protecting those resources? Well, it still basically comes down to states and that's why we have so much invested in sovereignty. Still, we're afraid to give sovereignty up because if we give it up, what happens? Are we then even more insecure? So we cling to what we've had, namely sovereignty, because we don't know how to build the alternative—the bridge to the future.

I think that we've missed opportunities to start building the global architecture of the future. Hopefully, we can begin addressing a long-term institutional capacity. Today, we're talking a lot about Iraqi institutions. Now, we need to think globally about the global commons. That's a long-term enterprise. If we start now, the project will be passed on to later generations, if we are so fortunate to still have generations able to live on this planet.

J. GRAYZEL: Would you agree?

Danger of Imposed Religion and Values

C. NEWMAN: I do, but I don't want to get too far away from something that was said earlier that's probably not going to make me too popular. The missing element is the ethics, the values, that's true. What I am very nervous about is how that gap gets filled. I say I'm nervous about this because it's often filled by "arrogant" religion. That's very dangerous. I recognize that religion and values are missing in almost everything we do. It's the reason why the wealthier we are, the less we give. It's the reason why we walk past someone who needs help and we don't help them. But I want to be careful about how we address that problem. I don't know what the answer is, but I do worry if we move from being a secular world government, a secular national government, then it's a question of *whose* set of values and *whose* religion is in control? Once that's determined, then it becomes a competition and it becomes very dangerous. So the concept of equality doesn't have the same meaning if a

...I do worry if we move from being a secular world government, a secular national government, then it's a question of whose set of values and whose religion is in control? Once that's determined, then it becomes a competition and it becomes very dangerous.

particular religious group is in control.

J. GRAYZEL: Dr. Manocha?

Unity of Science and Religion

K. MANOCHA: Connie [Newman] has raised a very pertinent and very important point. We've yet to determine the place of religion in public life. Unfortunately, the voices we hear the most, who speak the loudest, are those on either end of the spectrum—the extremists, extreme proponents who would have us follow one path and impose it, unfortunately, through violent means—and those at the other end who would ditch the whole thing altogether, who see no place for faith-based values in society. Both ends of that spectrum, both those points of view, both those attitudes don't promote a sustainable, peaceful society and we need to recognize that.

We always need to recognize that there is the entire body of humanity's religious experience to draw on. I understand that the Bahá'í Chair[17] has been promoting an understanding of the spiritual heritage of mankind—that entire body of values, of insight into human nature, into what truly motivates the human being and gives shape and fullness to the human life. Those values are there; those principles are there to be drawn on and to be examined and applied. I think that the question of religion can't be divorced from its coupling with science—the principle of the harmony between science and religion. This interplay between these two great sources of knowledge needs to be better understood and appreciated in society.

I think that the question of religion can't be divorced from its coupling with science— the principle of the harmony between science and religion. This interplay between these two great sources of knowledge needs to be better understood and appreciated in society.

---

[17] The Bahá'í Chair for World Peace at the University of Maryland, the sponsoring organization of the Interactive Dialogue.

To manage Iraq successfully, I would do the following. One, reinstall the monarchy, the king, who governed Iraq under a constitutional monarchy starting in 1921 until the coup d'état of 1958.

Yes, religion is not just about esoteric elucidations, statements of the exotic. It's actually statements of the reality of who we are—aspirational statements about the way we ought to be. We should be rigorous, scientific, and practical. We should look at how we can apply these to our individual lives and the life of society and actually go back and learn from that experience and evaluate that experience. Do these things actually work? I think we should use the methodology of science to demonstrate the eternal validity of these very important and very powerful and transformative spiritual principles and values. Then we have a way out of this scenario, which is not entirely helpful because there isn't common agreement and common consensus of how we move forward and we clearly do need to move forward.

J. GRAYZEL: Dr. al-Moumin, I want to ask you a question of a type I call: "If you can answer it, you win the Nobel Peace Prize." One of the things I learned in my life working with people is that one of the things we have to break out of is thinking that we are helping the "other." In fact, all over the world there are wise people who actually have much counsel to give to us. If we went back to Day Two after the U.S. occupation of Iraq, what approach would you have recommended? How would you take the statements you just heard? Are they realistic? How would you have put them into action?

King and Community in Iraq

M. AL-MOUMIN: Well, are you ready? If it was up to me and I had to make a decision on Day Two, I would choose between two options. To manage Iraq successfully, I would do the following. One, reinstall the monarchy, the king, who governed Iraq under a constitutional monarchy starting in 1921 until the coup d'état of 1958. The king was a very unique figure in Iraq. He was a Sunni and a Shiite in one body. It was a constitutional monarchy, so the prime minister, the Cabinet, and the Parliament, all these figures were elected. The king was secular and respected, so he was the father figure who brought the entire society together.

The Middle East is a region founded on tribes, so you would naturally follow the leader. In the Middle East, people generally don't appreciate the nation, they appreciate the *leader*. If that leader changes every four years, people are distracted. I've been to many Middle Eastern countries, and the flag of the country doesn't get hung very often. Nobody hangs the flag, but they do hang the picture of the leader. Here in the United States, I went to almost all the states. In government offices, you hang the picture of the president. To operate in the Middle East, you have to speak the Middle Eastern "language."

If you don't do that, my second option for Iraq would be to empower the local, traditional leadership. So, community-based leadership is important. I would empower those traditional figures, rather than empowering politicians.[18] These would be my two options.

...my second option for Iraq would be to empower the local, traditional leadership.

J. GRAYZEL: Dr. Cronin, you've heard that recommendation, but you've also stressed the need to look at realities. I can't help being particularly touched by the problem you raised when you talked about piracy. I find that such an interesting phenomenon. First of all, if you listen to the U.S. Marine Corps hymn, we've dealt with pirates in

---

[18] See note 20 for the role that traditional clans have seemingly played in stabilizing Somaliland, an oasis of human security amid the choas of Somalia.

the eighteenth century on the Barbary Coast.[19] We're now in a situation off the coast of Somalia, where it appears to me that the Russians, the French, the Chinese, the Americans, and the British, are all actually willing, to a minimal degree, to cooperate to fight piracy; they all see this as a problem but are still cowed by a group of creative fishermen who have gotten their hands on some modern GPS technology. Is it realistic to expect us to actually engineer solutions anymore or is there something very different we have to start thinking about doing?

Learning the Limits of External Intervention

P. CRONIN: A few thoughts. One of them—starting with Iraq and thinking of my friend Tom Ricks' successful book, *Fiasco*, which describes the early years of the U.S. presence in Iraq. The book reminds us of the need for great humility. As any external power going abroad to do anything, to think that you're going to do more than play some kind of supportive role—unless you're going to permanently occupy the place—you're deluding yourself very badly. If you're not going to have a UN mandate and completely conquer a place, which is what we don't do anymore, you'd better take into account the local traditions, cultures, norms, and what Ambassador Jim Dobbins calls the "neighborhood rule." In other words, you want a government that's at least as capable and competent as the neighborhood in which the people live.

As any external power going abroad to do anything, to think that you're going to do more than play some kind of supportive role—unless you're going to permanently occupy the place—you're deluding yourself very badly.

---

[19] In honor of its early campaigns, the official U.S. Marine Corps hymn begins with the lines, "From the Halls of Montezuma, to the shores of Tripoli...." The "shores of Tripoli" is a reference to the 1805 action in which Marines attacked and captured a fortress (located on what is now the coast of modern-day Libya) held by Barbary pirates.

Top-Down Solutions Fail

On Somalia, we repeat the same practice: the U.S. government waits for a crisis and then reacts and then we try to impose top-down solutions without thinking of more traditional, comprehensive solutions. Now those comprehensive solutions are not very easy. They're vying desperately for attention and resources with other items on the agenda, and that agenda gets very crowded. So, we end up waiting for a crisis. We then once again try a top-down solution without thinking of how do we reduce the problem set, because the key questions are, "Where's the piracy coming from? What are the roots of the piracy? What are the roots of political violence and conflict in Somalia? Why has it just been voted the worst state on the planet?"

Somalia is a failed state—a classic case of it—and yet you can reduce the problem of Somalia. You can think about the Puntland and Somaliland[20]

On Somalia, we repeat the same practice: the U.S. government waits for a crisis and then reacts and then we try to impose top-down solutions without thinking of more traditional, comprehensive solutions.

---

[20] Puntland and Somaliland are regions located in the north and northwest of Somalia, respectively. Following the collapse of the government of Somalia in 1991, both achieved effective separation (Somaliland in 1991 and Puntland in 1998), but no other country has formally recognized their claims of independence.

For a profile of Somaliland on the eve of a presidential election, see Jeffrey Gettleman, "Carving Out a Slice of Democracy in Somalia," *New York Times*, 25 June 2010 (available from [http://www.nytimes.com/2010/06/26/world/africa/26somaliland.html]; accessed 25 June 2010). Interestingly, Gettleman suggests that Somaliland's success in delivering human security—including genuine democracy—to its population is linked to the durability of the region's traditional social structure:

"In many respects, Somaliland is already its own country, with its own currency, its own army and navy, its own borders and its own national identity....Part of this stems from its distinct colonial history, having been ruled, relatively indirectly, by the British, while the rest of Somalia was colonized by the Italians, who set up a European administration.

"Italian colonization supplanted local elders, which may have been one reason why much of Somalia plunged into clan-driven chaos after 1991, while Somaliland succeeded in reconciling its clans."

For the role that Iraq's traditional, local leadership might play in stabilizing that country, see the text corresponding to note 18.

as more stable, possibly governable areas. Now you've reduced the geographic area and if you can think about sustaining the maritime commons with an international regime—it's right now a *de facto* regime—that's real cooperation. The Chinese were looking after only Chinese ships but, nonetheless, there's growing international cooperation against piracy. But you have to persist, not just when the pirates are attacking, but after the lull, when they start attacking again. Unfortunately, it's a vast sea and coastline off Somalia, where pirates can strike and they have more technological capability to get out beyond the shore and create problems. But if we're going to have a lasting solution, it's going to take a more comprehensive stabilization of the Somali state.

So, where are the resources, where is the political will? How much can we do as external powers? Can we think of a bottom-up and a top-down approach, because that's what it's going to take? It's going to take both of those and it's going to take time. You have to build institutions. You're absolutely right. You have to have water, electricity, and so on, but if you're going to sustain the security in any geographical area to make sure the water stays on and the electricity stays on, you're going to be building an institution, unless you're going to be stationed there permanently.

Bureaucratic Politics and Clashing Timeframes

And institution-building is not something you can just provide overnight. It is something that has to be grown up and adjusted to, and that's going to take time. It's that time frame that we don't do well in Washington. It's the timeframe of USAID versus the Pentagon; it's the timeframe of the National Security Council versus the development

And institution-building is not something you can just provide overnight. It is something that has to be grown up and adjusted to, and that's going to take time. It's that time frame that we don't do well in Washington.

world. Those are constantly in clash. So how do we take this long, broad perspective?

Values and the Policy Process

How do we infuse our secular policy decisions, rule-based systems even, with a moral imperative? I take Connie [Newman's] point as very important. Believe me, if you allow religion to seep into our policy directly, you may regret what you wished for, because the religion favored may not be yours.

Anne-Marie Slaughter has written very eloquently about this.[21] She's now the director of policy planning at the state department. She has written very eloquently about trying to tap into American values. It's very important to be true to those values, but not to impose those values on others and not to impose yours alone on the process. To create a rules-based system, that's ultimately what we're trying to build, so we want freedom of religion, but we don't want our religion projected on everybody else. It's the freedom of religion and freedom to speak, and it's those universal freedoms enshrined in the Declaration of Human Rights, for instance, that can be a shared set of values.

J. GRAYZEL: I'm going to ask two more questions, and then if there are questions from the audience, we will begin to answer them. What Dr. Cronin presents sounds very logical. Then I go back and say, "Is it that we don't do this because we don't understand the logic, or is it that we ourselves have an insecurity that actually paralyzes us from logically doing things? And, if so, how do we overcome that paralysis?"

How do we infuse our secular policy decisions, rule-based systems even, with a moral imperative?... Believe me, if you allow religion to seep into our policy directly, you may regret what you wished for, because the religion favored may not be yours.

---

[21] Anne-Marie Slaughter, *The Idea that Is America: Keeping Faith with Our Values in a Dangerous World* (New York: Basic Books, 2007).

Negatives of Perpetual Insecurity

C. NEWMAN: We have insecurity as a nation and that is encouraged, for business and political reasons, because defense is big business. I know I'm being very cynical, but I'm just saying that there's a great deal of money and a great deal on the line in order to "make this country secure." In order to support that stance, there has to be a lot of talk that makes us feel *insecure*. When we feel insecure, we accept a lot of things that basically are not moral.[22] We can get into "why torture?" Well, torture was more accepted because for many reasons we felt more insecure and we argued that we needed to get information from these folks so that we could be more secure. I'm being circular here, so I'm not excusing this, but I've been trying to understand. Why is it that wealthy nations do not do more for development?

---

[22] The phenomenon cited by Secretary Newman—a willful overemphasis on security leading to a sense of morbid insecurity resulting in self-harming actions—is also addressed by the historian John Lukacs in the following critique of U.S. foreign policy during the Cold War: "The leaders of the Soviet Union were neither modest nor pacifist. But their most startling acts of intervention were made because of purposes that were defensive; they had more troubles of their own than people suspected or were willing to admit; their appetite for more foreign expansion and conquest was something quite different from being insatiable. With all the technological and analytical information at their disposal, people in charge of the enormous bureaucratic labyrinths in Washington—along with experts and, increasingly, intellectuals in high government positions—either did not see these things at all or surely not clearly enough. Worse when people do not see something, this often means that they do not wish to see it—a condition that may be comfortable and profitable to them. That was true of many of our presidents during the Cold War, from Eisenhower to Reagan; of popular political figures, from Joe McCarthy to Oliver North; and of experts such as Henry Kissinger, who began his grand public career by touting the existence of a—as we now know, nonexistent—Missile Gap. Consequently, the Cold War lasted longer than it should have, and the United States became transformed into the very military-industrial state the prospect of which in 1960 a speechwriter put in one of Eisenhower's last public speeches—the end

This whole debate that we're having on health care is a debate we shouldn't be having. There shouldn't be people on the streets pushing carts. That shouldn't be happening in a wealthy nation. So why is that happening? Some of it is the gap in convincing us that we are, or should be, our brother's keeper. I don't know where that gap came from because I think all of us, when we grew up, were told that we should give back, but we don't do it. Or we rationalize. There's a lot of rationalizing—lack of honesty—in how we deal with one another and how we deal as communities and nations. We justify our behavior.

J. GRAYZEL: Dr. Manocha, this is a question that I hear from many of my students. Beyond all that is said, as to the systematic explanation of why things are happening, if we don't want something to be the case, we have to change it. If we want

---

result being that while it is not now arguable that the Soviet Union lost the Cold War, it may be arguable whether the United States has won it." See Lukacs, "The End of the Twentieth Century: Historical Reflections on a Misunderstood Epoch," *Harper's Magazine*, January 1993 (available from Academic Search Premier database).

The book *Apocalypse Management: Eisenhower and the Discourse of National Insecurity* (Palo Alto, CA: Stanford University Press, 2008), by the scholar Ira Chernus, reinforces the interpretations of Newman and Lukacs. "The Eisenhower presidency," writes Chernus (p. 11), "locked the nation into the cold war's enduring paradox: A single-minded pursuit of national security consistently undermined the nation's sense of security." For a somewhat critical review of *Apocalypse Management*, see Saki R. Dockrill, "The Language of the New Look," *Diplomatic History* 34 (June 2010): 615-18.

Finally, professors Campbell Craig and Fredrik Logevall comprehensively address the security-insecurity theme in their study *America's Cold War: The Politics of Insecurity* (Cambridge: Harvard University Press, 2009). A thoughtful exchange on this book can be found in Stephen J. Whitefield, Andrew J. Falk, Julian E. Zelizer, Kyle Longley, Campbell Craig and Fredrick Logevall, "A Roundtable Discussion of Campbell Craig and Fredrik Logevall's *America's Cold War: The Politics of Insecurity*," in *Passport* (Newsletter of the Society for Historians of American Foreign Relations) 41 (September 2010): 26-27, 31-33, 35-39.

things to change, it has to be individuals who change them, and themselves. So, the question is, while on one level the fear of getting into battles over values, morals, and religion is warranted—perhaps from your work in psychiatry—how do we get the individual motivated to enact the change that has to happen?

Motivating Individuals

K. MANOCHA: It's a very good question. I wish I knew the answer. I think one of the things that individuals do well is they know what needs to be done. They know, for example, if they're seeing a psychiatrist or psychotherapist that the way to live a better life is to block out the negative thoughts. Where they don't do so well is actually blocking out the negative thoughts. You sit there and they come back to you week in and week out with the same old negative assumptions about themselves, the way the world is, and how powerless they are. And you say, "Now do it; just do it." There has to be a recognition somewhere within them that now is the time to do it. Walk that path and see how far you get and see what life is like on the other side.

So I think when it comes to individuals, they have to want change; they have to have a compelling vision of what they can do, the way the world could be; the way society should be; they have to own it at a very, very deep level—it's not at an intellectual level—it has to be at a level that touches their spirit, their core, their being; and then they have to do it.

Now, sometimes it helps to have someone or someones to model after—to actually see how that life could be; how that society could be; what that world could look like. This is where working together with others and finding a system to consult, to make decisions, to reach common understandings can be extremely motivating, powerful, and effective to get people to make those decisions to cross over and to be a force for change and good.

I think when you identify fundamental principles in life which lead to practical solutions, then you have the beginnings of a sustainable process and you build into that other ways of reflecting on your experiences and you move along in that direction, but at some stage a person has to really want to allow themselves to be influenced to be a source of good, of change, and an agent for promoting the very best of civilization.

J. GRAYZEL: I have to get to some audience questions and they're always very good. However, there is some overlap so please forgive me if I paraphrase some of the questions. The first one, which I think is very interesting, is "What role, beneficial or dangerous, does the rapid change in the reality of communication around the world pose for us?" To what extent does this phenomenon itself pose such an important alteration of reality that we have to look at it more carefully? We have to really decide when it is beneficial or is it not beneficial and how do we manage it. Or do we just keep it a *laissez faire* situation?

More Information Is Not Better Information

C. NEWMAN: First of all, the genie is out of the bottle. In other words, we're going to have to learn how to manage it. It's already where it is and it's moving fast and further. I think we need to learn some things: how to manage it and make it higher quality. There's so much that moves, there's no quality control. We need to learn how to make it available to all people because for now, there's a poverty line of communication and that means that there are groups of people who will never be able to compete unless they're brought into the Information Age.

So, I just think that smart people need to figure out how to better ensure quality of communication. Some of the problem with communication is not that it's there, but it's that nobody checks the facts. One of the sad things is that newspapers used to use three sources before they printed anything. The Internet and bloggers, they don't use any sources at all. They say they do, but I don't really believe they do. We need to have some of that regulated. And then, I think we need to figure out how do we make information available to more people so that there is a democracy in the exchange of information.

P. CRONIN: Building on that and maybe extending it, I think the information revolution has come and will continue to be part of the ubiquity of information that's with us, even if not evenly. One of Connie Newman's points was this digital divide that exists in a place like Sub-Saharan Africa, where there may be a lot of mobile telephones and a few benefit economically, but without greater dissemination and availability of information there can't be wider economic opportunity in a globalized economy, so that is a problem at one dimension.

Connie also mentioned the need for better quality, and I think you can expand that to talk about the need for differentiating between information that students at the University of Maryland will have access to when they Google versus *knowledge*, which if they're lucky they may hear from some of my colleagues tonight. Knowledge is something that's harder to acquire. One of the things we don't do is reflection. So, I'm tied to my Blackberry tonight. I may have to look for an e-mail, but the point is, where do we reflect?

Some of the problem with communication is not that it's there, but it's that nobody checks the facts.

Where do we contemplate? Where do we figure out what's truly important and fashion strategies in response?

Information Systems and Insecurity

There are two other dimensions here. Let me go back to security. Modern developed societies are particularly vulnerable now because they have centralized their systems. Don't believe that doesn't affect you. It doesn't necessarily just affect the Pentagon's computers. It also affects your identity through identity theft, as we know. If there's no secrets, that's one problem for the Pentagon, but if you have no way of possessing your identity, that's a problem for you as well. Your bank account could be emptied by the time you get home.

Communication and Mobilization

Then there's a more positive issue here that cuts both ways. It's communications technology for social mobilization. Each individual today— everybody in this room has the capacity to mobilize other people in a way we've never had before through communication. Now Osama bin Laden would like to mobilize certain types of people in one way, so this can have a dark edge, but there are also many positive advances because you can now reach from this community beyond whatever we write in the report of this dialogue and it can be disseminated. So you can mobilize communities for action and you can take that individual action, if you're motivated, and you can mobilize it. And you're going to have to, by the way, because a lot of what we're trying to do is to build new forms of governance to try to deal with this complex world we're living in. That's going to take cooperation.

Then there's a more positive issue here that cuts both ways. It's communications technology for social mobilization. Each individual today—everybody in this room has the capacity to mobilize other people in a way we've never had before through communication.

Engaged Citizenry

K. MANOCHA: To build on that point, unfortunately, governments left to their own devices often don't do the right thing. They need to be sustained by citizens, by enlightened, progressive citizens who are able to think critically and imaginatively about the way the world can be and are committed to building that world. The technology we have at our disposal can mobilize millions of individuals in different contexts in raising their voices to support processes that are conducive to a peaceful and better world.

So, technology, despite all the potential pitfalls that exist, and we should be very clear about them and address them, has an extraordinary benefit. And one can't help but think that it has come at the right time in the history of humanity, to make this transition between the way the world is and the world we're aspiring to build. We're not just talking about human security, but, ultimately, global security—a secure global order. We know from our own experience of our body that the health of the part is best served by the health of the whole. You can't have human security being a divisible thing. You can't compartmentalize it. The body of nations has to be secure to ensure that individuals and communities *within* the body of nations are secure.

M. AL-MOUMIN: I think the rapid change in communication challenges us all to become more communicative—to have effective messages that can reach broader audiences. When we write an e-mail, when we tweet on Twitter, we have limited space, so we have to be effective to reach a broader audience. I think that rapid change challenges us all the time to become more efficient and more effective.

We're not just talking about human security, but, ultimately, global security.... You can't have human security being a divisible thing. You can't compartmentalize it. The body of nations has to be secure to ensure that individuals and communities within the body of nations are secure.

J. GRAYZEL: [Reading questions submitted in writing by audience members] The trouble with bright students is that they don't let you get away with things. I've got a couple of very specific questions, so let's try to answer them, however hard they are. [Addressing Mishkat al-Moumin] The first one has to do with a combination of what you said. You talked about the need to provide things for people—basic services and so on. But someone says, "Given the reality of life, if you provide these things but then they are"—and I'm paraphrasing—"captured by groups that aren't positive." So the recommendation becomes, "meet the needs of people," but there seem to be some really smart people out there who seem to be ahead of government. How do we deal with that?

Empowering Communities

M. AL-MOUMIN: You empower the people to meet their needs. You don't do it for them. You empower them, build their capacity so they can do it themselves. I worked in Sadr City [in Baghdad] many, many times and I helped provide basic needs. However, I empowered people to do it themselves, rather than me doing it for them. First of all, I reached out to them and built a trust with them. So, there was a civil society connection between the people and the Ministry of Environment. Everyone was involved in the process—local NGOs, clerics, community leaders, and they helped in providing the needs of people. In the early stage, the Ministry helped finance the process and helped provide these needs. Later on, people started doing things for themselves. The level of violence was really reduced after implementing these programs.

The other outcome that I've noticed was that Sunni and Shiite people came together. It was a positive by-product of what we were doing. They said, "We all need safe drinking water." So, now when we talk about national reconciliation in Iraq and it's not progressing, the reason is because "my" national interest is the exact opposite of "yours." So there is no minimum way for us to meet. But we do meet wonderfully when we try to meet everyone's basic environmental needs. You need water, I need water, we can work together on it.

The other interesting outcome I noticed when working with my NGO—an organization on women and the environment—the gender gap was bridged in the traditional, local community and among people by using the environmental theme. So, we built the capacity of women to participate in environmental decision-making in local communities. And the community was very comfortable with this process. In fact, they supported the effort. So, there are themes that can unify us. There are other themes that divide us.

The easy way to implement positive change is to do it through people and with them, rather than doing it for them.

J. GRAYZEL: [Reading questions submitted in writing by audience members] I have a number of questions that I will distill into five. First, "What can I do?" Second, "What can we do on the grassroots level in terms of ensuring human security worldwide?" Third, "How can we do it nonviolently?" Fourth, "How can we do it when either we have government structures that really do more to block than to promote?" Fifth, "How can we get our military strategists to consider non-violent solutions that might answer our security needs better?" Can you begin, Dr. Cronin?

So, now when we talk about national reconciliation in Iraq and it's not progressing, the reason is because "my" national interest is the exact opposite of "yours." So there is no minimum way for us to meet. But we do meet wonderfully when we try to meet everyone's basic environmental needs.

U.S. Military and Non-Violent Solutions

P. CRONIN: Let's start with the last one and some of the ways we can have the military think about alternative approaches. One way is to encourage the idea of conflict *prevention*. When we get into interagency meetings, rather than thinking about how do we prosecute the crisis *du jour*, we need to be thinking about what are the foreign policy objectives that we have to try to project and how do we work with others and mobilize the international community, mobilize local actors, to try to prevent the conflict from spreading, or breaking out in the first place? How do we then use our development tools to help stabilize and build institutions? That's the first thing we don't do enough of because we do too much crisis management and not enough long-term planning. We can't do it on our own at all. So we have to let go and work and cooperate with others. We're starting to see a lot of that approach from the Obama administration, but it's very tough to make that actually happen.

In conflicts themselves, as we see, we can choose to ignore Afghanistan, but Afghanistan is an ongoing war. So General McChrystal[23] goes in and writes his twelve rules so that every soldier has to say, including: "I can't just go and indiscriminately use force; in fact, my whole idea is not to use force; in fact, the best thing I may do is not to respond to an attack." That's a start towards understanding the political purpose of using force. It was Mao who actually said that you can never divorce, for even an instant, war from a political purpose. It was Karl von Clausewitz who talked about this admixture,

How do we then use our development tools to help stabilize and build institutions? That's the first thing we don't do enough of because we do too much crisis management and not enough long-term planning.

---

[23] General Stanley A. McChrystal, the senior Western military commander in Afghanistan (leading U.S. forces in the country as well as the International Security Assistance Force [ISAF]) from June 2009 to June 2010.

how war is nothing but politics by other means.

There has to be a political objective here and the objective is actually to provide peace and prosperity. It is to try to protect human security. So, if you inculcate that within your military leaders, change can happen, non-violent solutions can be implemented. Some military leaders, like David Petraeus,[24] actually understand this, but he's then given a mission that he has to prosecute. So he's not given autonomy, he has to work within very tight boundaries, but he understands the concept in general that we're here to protect people, so he can start to do that.

What Can Individuals Do?

Now let me address the first question you posed. How do we start to do something even if we're not at the National Security Council or not working for General Petraeus' brain trust? Well, there are a million ways. It's called civil society on the outside. Civil society has advanced in all sorts of ways. Read the work of Peter Ackerman on civil resistance,[25] which has led to a lot of peaceful resistance. The civil society approach builds on Gandhi, on the "color revolutions" of the post-Soviet era.[26]

There has to be a political objective here and the objective is actually to provide peace and prosperity. It is to try to protect human security. So, if you inculcate that within your military leaders, change can happen, non-violent solutions can be implemented.

---

[24] General David H. Petraeus, commander of the United States Central Command (CENTCOM), which includes responsibility for Iraq and Afghanistan. General Petraeus was "demoted" when, in June 2010, President Obama asked him to succeed General McChrystal as commander ISAF (see previous note).

[25] Peter Ackerman and Jack Duvall, *A Force More Powerful: A Century of Nonviolent Conflict* (New York: Palgrave, 2000).

[26] "Color revolutions" is the collective term applied to a series of distinct mass protest movements that employed similar non-violent strategies to achieve political change in their respective national politics. Georgia, for example, experienced a "Rose Revolution" in 2003, while Ukraine underwent an "Orange Revolution" the following year.

The nature and significance of these movements is captured in the following description of a March 2005 protest that occurred in Bei-

The civil society approach builds on a lot of other experiences, including even the Civil Rights movement here in the United States. You can work for non-governmental organizations and you can decide which ones, through the Internet, are doing a better job than others and that are more effectively trying to pursue these objectives. A lot of small NGOs can do good but, unfortunately, they can also do harm. When I was in Liberia I was told that a particular religious institution was rife with corruption—they couldn't trust the staff with one dollar from one end of the hall of this church to the other end of the hall. So, corruption was part of the way of survival in the early stages of rebuilding Liberia. Now they've actually done amazing things in a short period of time.

Can we sustain that type of work on the ground? Well, that's going to take civil society because governments don't have the attention span or resources to keep focused on it. So there are lots of ways to involve yourself that actually make a big difference in human security. You don't even have to go abroad. You can go right here in Washington, DC and make a difference on human security.

Change Begins with Incremental Steps

C. NEWMAN: Some of creating change is about attitudes, and this is what I mean. Everybody in this room knows of a place where they can

Can we sustain that type of work on the ground? Well, that's going to take civil society because governments don't have the attention span or resources to keep focused on it.

rut, the central event and defining moment of what came to be called Lebanon's "Cedar Revolution": "Never before have we seen anything like it in Lebanon. Never before have we seen anything like it in the Arab world. Almost a third of the population of Lebanon was there; they walked many miles through the city to Martyrs' Square, they arrived by bus from the far north and from Sidon in the south, most of them young, many of them children....This was not just a game of power. Nor was it, per se, a democratic revolution. It was an insurrection by the people against the lies and corruption of govern- ment as well as the foreign control they have lived under for so many decades." See Robert Fisk, "Cry Goes Out for Freedom in Beirut's Martyrs' Square," *The Independent*, 15 March 2005, p. 24.

serve. Everybody could take one brick and add it to another brick that already exists and make a difference. What is often the problem is our expectation and hope that we're going to make a major difference and we're looking for that one place where we're going to see a major change because of what we do. But change comes incrementally. It is boring, often. I worked in migrant camps for years. Now there was nothing that I was doing in those migrant camps that made a difference in terms of national policy, except that later, after having worked in migrant camps, I became a leader in an agency that funded migrant farm workers. So what I'm saying to the students is that they can look out their window, often, and see a place to make a small difference, if their attitude is that they're satisfied with that for the time being because it will lead to their ability to make larger differences.

Roméo Dallaire on the Oneness of Humanity

K. MANOCHA: One of the most inspiring people I've ever had the good fortune to know and to work with is Senator Roméo Dallaire, who was the commander of the UN mission in Rwanda during genocide of 1994. In reflecting on his experiences in that hell, he made a very critical point. He said, "It took that experience to impress upon my mind, on my heart, the fundamental oneness of the human family." Now we cannot afford to learn that lesson through those horrors again, so he dedicated himself to speaking to audiences, particularly in universities and colleges about the genocide and to ask the question of those individuals that he speaks to: "What are the lessons to be learned from this experience?" And when the analysis is at the level of high politics, he is angry and frustrated, because the salient lesson has not been learned or picked up.

One of the most inspiring people I've ever had the good fortune to know and to work with is Senator Roméo Dallaire, who was the commander of the UN mission in Rwanda during genocide of 1994.

I think that in that spirit, if you like, the salient point in terms of how we can advance human security is for us to be empowered to advance and implement the process of the oneness of the human family, upon which this whole edifice, this whole order we are constructing, in terms of a better world, depends. It's a principle that should fashion international affairs.

I think there's one practical thing that anyone can really do, and that is to understand that value—the oneness of humanity—and to align oneself with that value. But most of all, teach it to the young people. If you want to do one particular service, teach it to the children and the junior youth because their minds are fresh and their attitudes haven't yet been formed and they can pick up this principle; they can internalize it, and they can recreate society as a result. That will lead to extraordinary long-term benefit for mankind.

Roméo Dallaire and the Prevention of Genocide

P. CRONIN: I'd like to share a personal note on Roméo Dallaire. I second, certainly, his heroism, but I knew him before the Rwanda mission because he had come to the National Defense University at Fort McNair. At that time we were trying to mobilize political opinion to get more political support so that the United Nations would put enough troops to provide security in the refugee camps. We failed to do that. After the genocide, Roméo Dallaire had a nervous breakdown. He slept on benches, he was a broken man. So there are a couple of lessons from that. One of them is simply that as you get involved in these issues, they are not hazard-free. Just like that development system is going to create winners and losers, it's also going to shake you and from his experience, he got off that bench. He wrote a

I think there's one practical thing that anyone can really do, and that is to understand that value— the oneness of humanity—and to align oneself with that value.

book. He has become a force for good. He has helped to mobilize a great deal of political action to help prevent genocide in the future.

The Individual in a Network

M. AL-MOUMIN: What can we do to bring about change? Spread the word about it. Tell people about it. You can go on Facebook and ask a question about it. You can go on Twitter and tweet about it. You can reach out to the next-door neighbor and see if she or he thinks like you. The grassroots level movement always starts by reaching out to people who think like us or have the same values or acknowledge the same principle, and then the movement grows and grows until it becomes a force for change.

I'm fascinated by the protests in Iran. The whole thing started through Twitter and people were mobilized by that. Acknowledgement is so important. Acknowledging the value or acknowledging the approach to the problem is the first step to address the issue.

Innovative Approaches to Security

I'll give you two examples, two real case studies. So, in Iraq we don't have electricity all the time. When electricity goes down, oftentimes, you have it one hour and the rest of the day you are without. So, with time on their hands, young people start going to mosques because mosques have back-up generators. However, while at the mosque they receive indoctrination on becoming jihadists and blowing themselves up. The traditional approach to security is that you surround the mosque and you kick everybody out and you arrest people and put them in jail. However, this approach results in threatening security because you are validating the

The grassroots level movement always starts by reaching out to people who think like us or have the same values or acknowledge the same principle, and then the movement grows and grows until it becomes a force for change.

claims of insurgents. So, you need an innovative approach to security. How can you address this issue as a human security issue by providing this basic need—the need for electricity and energy?

Another case study I came across is a crime committed in Egypt: a man killed his brother because he spent one hour in the bathroom. They only had one bathroom in the house, and the brother who was killed spent more time than he should in it. The other brother was frustrated over his basic need all the time. The victim came out, they had an argument, and one brother killed the other. Now how should investigators deal with this issue? Do you consider that person a criminal, same as the one who committed a crime because he killed somebody and took his money? You can't. So we need to start by acknowledging the issue, acknowledging the problem and adopt an innovative approach towards it.

J. GRAYZEL: Our time is quickly coming to a close, so I want to ask three final, provocative questions—two from the audience and then my own. The first one is: In the end—this is a paraphrase of two questions—doesn't it begin and end with justice, and justice for the individual? How do we assure minimal justice for people who we expect to act in the rational ways you just described? And if we don't, can we really make any progress?

The person posing the question doesn't give an example, so let me give one. Just recently, soldiers of the government of Guinea raped hundreds of women in a public stadium. Yet it is still a recognized government by the international community. So if we can't actually provide individual justice, does it mean anything to just talk nobly about world justice?

So, you need an innovative approach to security. How can you address this issue as a human security issue by providing this basic need—the need for electricity and energy?

Peace and Justice Inseparable?

K. MANOCHA: I can't see how we would expect to ever build a secure world without giving due attention a fundamental principle of life, which is justice. It's not to say that we haven't made huge efforts over centuries, of millennia, to fashion this principle, but it's going to require from us huge efforts to fashion structures, processes that administer justice. We have to internalize that balance within ourselves. We have to know how that looks in terms of our own individual relationships and how, if you like, our interests—the interests of the individual—are inextricably linked with the interests of society. That is one of the things that justice ultimately teaches us. And we need to find mechanisms of consultation and decision-making that lead to just outcomes and decisions.

I think these are deeply moral and spiritual matters. Yes, it does take legal forms; it crystallizes into legal norms, but these are moral issues for individuals to work through, and for communities to work through, and for nations to work through, and for the body of nations to work through.

C. NEWMAN: Let me address this on two levels. The first one is justice within communities, states, and nations. That comes about if there's real participation by citizens in governance. The only way you ensure that judges are not appointed because they're going to follow the political leadership is to have citizen participation. In this country, it's the confirmation process, which is citizen participation. You might argue that some people got appointed who shouldn't have gotten appointed and vice versa, but it does help bring about a justice system that people can rely on.

I can't see how we would expect to ever build a secure world without giving due attention a fundamental principle of life, which is justice.

Empowering the United Nations

But the more difficult question is the international question. You mentioned Guinea, but it's also Darfur. It was Rwanda. These situations require the nations to empower the United Nations to act. If we go back and look at each one of these cases—the Congo, Darfur, others—there should have been more power within the United Nations to act. If the veto power of Russia and China did not exist, there would have been a greater ability on the part of the international community to stop the genocide in Darfur.

What I'm saying is that justice exists when there's citizen participation and when there's citizen power. There has to be, on the international scene, more power in the hands of our international organizations. Let's not talk about starting from scratch. We've got the UN. We need to make the UN work. I just think that there needs to be more commitment on the part of the major powers, including the U.S., to engage with the UN and to ensure that the UN has power. If the U.S. holds back on its funding of the UN, it reduces the UN's ability to act. Yes, that's a way of ensuring that the UN does what we want them to do, but is that often in the best interests of the world? That's the question.

J. GRAYZEL: Dr. al-Moumin, do you have any comments on this?

Challenging Sovereignty

M. AL-MOUMIN: I would say we need to review the concept of sovereignty. Because oftentimes a state raises that flag—what happens inside my borders is *my* business. However, I think the time has come when we need to acknowledge

...we need to review the concept of sovereignty. Because oftentimes a state raises that flag—what happens inside my borders is my business.

that it's not that state's business only, it's the business of the entire world. There should be minimum standards that must be met. Now, I don't believe that at this stage in history that rape should occur, or genocide, or torture, or oppression, or any of these sort of things. It is time these ended. I believe it's time.

J. GRAYZEL: We're talking about new standards of sovereignty. How do you explain that to the congressional caucus when we can't even get standards for financial institutions? Is that realistic? Should we be striving for new standards of sovereignty? Or maybe it is happening and we're just not noticing it?

Complexity of Justice

P. CRONIN: You want realism or you want justice? Seriously, if we're talking about the United States political process, why is it so difficult to get change? Because most people are well-meaning. Most people inside the bureaucracy, most people inside Congress, most people in Wall Street were not necessarily corrupt. They were following rules, and culture, and standard operating procedures before the financial crisis. Some were Bernie Madoff and were crooks, so both were operating.

But how do we get change and justice? Justice is such an all-encompassing concept. Of course, justice is essential to our humanity. We're all bound eventually together by our own humanity. But injustice, though, can come about in so many different ways. So, there is no way to eradicate injustice, but we can reduce the space for injustice. We can create checks and balances, political processes. We can build institutions, globally and in terms of civil society, to help check this.

We're talking about new standards of sovereignty. How do you explain that to the congressional caucus when we can't even get standards for financial institutions?

...there is no way to eradicate injustice, but we can reduce the space for injustice. We can create checks and balances, political processes. We can build institutions, globally and in terms of civil society, to help check this.

Let's take Iraq. Where is injustice, not only today but tomorrow? Well, one of the big concerns is not just after the American troops leave. There are ethnic and sectarian differences in the country. There are Kurdish/Arab, and Shiite/Sunni, and it gets more complex than that. Basic differences, not to mention other countries in the neighborhood, which will create injustices, perpetuate injustices, encourage injustice.

So who's going to go in to Iraq and stop the injustice? It's not likely to be the United Nations as we've seen it, because there's been no enforcement mechanism, which is one of the good reasons why the United States has clung so much to its own power. It's because the U.S. believes it has a moral imperative to help provide global security. There are bad reasons, too, for U.S. behavior. Some of them go back, as Connie [Newman] mentioned, to the military industrial complex—something that President Dwight D. Eisenhower talked about as he was leaving the White House because we had created an entire service of the military around a technological military platform—the airplane. He was worried about it self-perpetuating itself, and it did. It did a pretty good job, actually, of perpetuating an Air Force. So that's a problem, too. It provided security, but it also created problems.

Politics of Foreign Assistance

So, on the legislative side, on development, I've talked to members of Congress and they say, "Listen, Patrick, we can't legitimately go to our constituents, who are now suffering through a recession." Last night, I had dinner with John McCain[27] at a function for people on both sides of

So who's going to go in to Iraq and stop the injustice? It's not likely to be the United Nations as we've seen it, because there's been no enforcement mechanism, which is one of the good reasons why the United States has clung so much to its own power.

---

[27] John McCain, a Republican member of the U.S. Senate from the State of Arizona and the 2008 Republican Party nominee for U.S. president.

the aisle. McCain has 18% unemployment in his state of Arizona. Now how does he go, even as a Senator—forget about members of the House of Representatives, who have more local concerns— and talk about increasing foreign assistance before he even takes care of the people in his own state? So what kind of assistance is he going to be bargaining for? If you're willing to put that down on child survival or something that clearly will resonate with a community, he'll fund that. But he's not going to fund discretionary money to go out and try to provide electricity and infrastructure and other things that may be required to allow a state or community to have sustainable development.

U.S. Habit of Unilateralism

Again, the United States can be a strategic catalyst. We cannot afford to try to do it alone. That's one of our problems, and it's true with our government all across the departments. We try to do it on our own and then add others only as an afterthought. It can't happen that way. Whatever we're doing, whether it's a humanitarian mission or post-conflict, or conflict prevention diplomacy, or just long-term development, we have to figure out ways to make our modest contribution have the biggest impact for promoting justice by promoting human development and human security.

J. GRAYZEL: It's getting late, but I would like to ask one last question. It's not one I prepared anyone for but what really makes me feel insecure is having to face my students tomorrow, and I know they'll ask me this question if you don't answer it first.

Whatever we're doing, whether it's a humanitarian mission or post-conflict, or conflict prevention diplomacy, or just long-term development, we have to figure out ways to make our modest contribution have the biggest impact for promoting justice by promoting human development and human security.

Moral Compass of Aristocrats and Believers

We talked about insecurity and about education and individual responsibility. What came to my mind was a very old but still germane book, *Man's Search for Meaning*, by Viktor Frankl.[28] If I remember correctly, Frankl talks about his experience in a Nazi concentration camp and how, obviously, most people were absolutely destroyed by being placed in that context. Certainly, a context as difficult as going back to your congressional district or having to deal with the bureaucracy or the U.S. Army, pales in comparison to being in a concentration camp. As I remember, what he pointed out was that despite that horror, there were people who didn't break down. There was a group of people who accepted their free will as being the decision they made, regardless of the

---

[28] Frankl's book was originally published in German in 1946 as ...*trotzdem Ja zum Leben sagen: Ein Psychologe erlebt das Konzentrationslager* ("...saying yes to life in spite of everything: A Psychologist Experiences the Concentration Camp"). The first English-language edition, published in 1959, was called *From Death-Camp to Existentialism*. In 1963, Frankl released a revised and expanded edition of his book (also translated from German) under what became its best-known English title, *Man's Search for Meaning*. To date, Frankl's influential work has been translated into more than twenty languages.

The role played by aristocrats, the religious, and other like-minded persons in resisting the Nazis has been noted by the historian John Lukacs: "...we must understand that in Germany (as elsewhere in Europe) the main and many of the most principled opponents of Hitler were traditionalists—believers in the patriotic, often religious, and above all moral and noble standards of an older and better world." Lukacs, 218 (see note 6 for full citation).

On the moral/religious motivations of the German anti-Nazi resistance, see also Hans Rothfels, *The German Opposition to Hitler*, rev. ed. (Chicago: Henry Regnery Company, 1962), especially pp. 12-13. Rothfels observes that aristocrats were "strongly represented in the conspiracy" (p. 12) against Hitler.

The participation of aristocrats in the German anti-Hitler movement is also discussed in Hans Mommsen, *Alternatives to Hitler: German Resistance under the Third Reich*, trans. Angus McGeoch (Princeton, NJ: Princeton University Press, 2003), 29-30, 45, 46-47, 48, 83-84.

circumstances they were in. Frankl says free will is precisely deciding what you can do between "right now" and "what next," given where you are.

The two groups, as I remember, that Frankl said had that sentiment were the very religious and the old aristocrats. It was the religious people and the aristocrats. Perhaps it does come back to the concept of the king, as in Iraq. We've talked about human security and we've talked about the need for water and sanitation and food, but these two groups had something else. They had a security in the core of their identity that none of the others in their situation seemed to have. But it seems that we've dismissed, to some extent, using these two tools—religion and aristocracy—because of our fear that they actually bring about conflict. I mean the conflict of hierarchy and power and the conflict of religious dogma and identity. And yet they have been, classically, the core of much of the most moral behavior in the world.

If you go down to our national monuments, people visit them but often they don't read the inscriptions. All of our leaders found a core values and higher meaning to their positions. So I'd like to ask each of you, beginning with Dr. Manocha: We can teach ideas, but don't we have to establish a true core, like those people Frankl wrote about had, that says "Regardless of the circumstances, this is my will and this is how I must act?" Can we get away with not doing that? And if we have to do it, how do we make people secure enough to have such strength? We don't use the tools of aristocracy anymore and we apparently are afraid to use religion, so what do we use? Or, alternatively, is there a new way of looking at religion and aristocracy that might allow us to reinvent them as appropriate in the twenty-first century?

...it seems that we've dismissed, to some extent, using these two tools—religion and aristocracy— because of our fear that they actually bring about conflict. I mean the conflict of hierarchy and power and the conflict of religious dogma and identity.

Freedom and Human Security

K. MANOCHA: We could happily spend an evening or a whole week of seminars and discussions like this to really get to the very heart of this, but what has been very encouraging in reviewing some of the reports that have come out of the United Nations in the last decade in terms of human development reports and other such documents, is a shift from a purely materialistic conception of human wellbeing and development to incorporating more systematically fundamental freedoms. One of the fundamental freedoms is the freedom and the right to believe and to think and to know. I think it all starts from that. If you're free to know, think, and believe and to change your belief and share your belief with others, then you're going to be in a position to begin to search for meaning, explore meaning, arrive at something that holds truth for you and then act on that and live that experience and, in that way, to seek fulfillment, which is the basis of your self-worth and dignity.

If you don't have self-worth and you don't have dignity and you don't have the right and the freedom to get to that place, then you could crumble. You would crumble in lesser circumstances than the horrors of a concentration camp or a civil war or whatever it is. But with that in place, yes, you then have the possibility and that is a commitment that governments absolutely must adhere to. You cannot derogate from that, because if you do, you rob humanity of its humanity and, actually, more than its humanity—it's very fundamental essence, which you can't put a value on.

Serving Humanity Close to Home

P. CRONIN: Let me revert to my nationalistic streak here and just talk about, as an American, why my families came from Europe 400 years ago

...what has been very encouraging in reviewing some of the reports that have come out of the United Nations in the last decade in terms of human development reports and other such documents, is a shift from a purely materialistic conception of human wellbeing and development to incorporating more systematically fundamental freedoms.

and 200 years ago to North America to get away from persecution. I don't think the aristocracy is going to speak to too many people in this audience, unless I've got you pegged wrong, so let's start with religion and maybe philosophy, at least, which we all have to have—a philosophy of life that, hopefully, is larger than ourselves, and understanding that we have a responsibility to protect the rights of others and their freedoms. How we go about that, whether through public service in civil society or in the government, international organizations, in our local community, in our schools, in our churches?

We have to be willing to live for something larger than ourselves and try to find ways to create justice and human security in our own communities. That's not always going to be something big like stopping World War III—it may be something much more mundane like Connie [Newman] was talking about—the day-to-day grind in migrant camps, where you don't see a big difference, but you know you're working toward a larger purpose and you're trying to hopefully make a difference with your life. I think we all have to find meaning in this way. We're all reduced to our humanity in this way. Death has a way of making us all equal, as Mark Twain once said.

So what are we going to achieve in our limited time? This is President Obama at the Great Wall of China imagining the sweep of history. We're nothing, if we can't make a difference during our lives. What are we going to be doing in our very short period here that can be larger than ourselves?

Local Networks for Human Security

M. AL-MOUMIN: Well, I'll share a story, since I'm a storyteller. In 2001, I was teaching at Baghdad University School of Law and I was asked to offer a topic, to offer a course—any course.

We have to be willing to live for something larger than ourselves and try to find ways to create justice and human security in our own communities.

There wasn't anything specific I was asked to do. So I chose to teach a class on human rights. I think that was a bit crazy because to teach human rights under a regime that has a long, dark history of systematic human rights abuses, that's really not a wise decision! Scared? I was terrified.

I spoke to my class and I asked the students, "What do you think of human rights?" I felt the students were afraid, too. Actually, they did not answer. However, throughout the course, we developed a strategy, without knowing that we did that. So, I'm adding my fear to their fears, but we are all finding a way to secure ourselves. For example, after one class some students followed me out of the room, saying, "Professor, be careful." I consider that really a brave thing to do.

Second of all, my students tried defending me, so when they were asked by the intelligence service, they would say, "No, she did not mean that. This is what she meant," which was really helpful. So when they provided this small and maybe insignificant contribution, it really made a big difference. In return, I supposedly should report to my department chairman, and I reported that the students are progressing. Look at the records, I said, they're doing fine. So, it was working both ways. I think adding your fears to other people's fears and finding a way to secure yourself can be something worth considering.

Inculcating Fairness

C. NEWMAN: Each of us has an obligation to pass on—whether it's to a child, grandchild, or whether it's a teacher to a student—the lessons, the values that are necessary to make society work in a fair way. I vaguely remember my parents leaning into the crib and saying to me, "First of all, life is short. It's not totally fair. You have an obligation

Each of us has an obligation to pass on—whether it's to a child, grandchild, or whether it's a teacher to a student—the lessons, the values that are necessary to make society work in a fair way.

to give back. There are bad things that are going to happen to you and how you're going to be judged is how you handle them." I think we need to teach that lesson. It's how I live, and I have to give back. It's not going to be totally fair, but what matters is how I handle what comes my way. And so, I thank you for allowing us to handle what has come our way this evening.

Conclusion

J. GRAYZEL: [Speaking to the panelists] I do want to thank all of you. What we do as part of the Interactive Dialogue is we take the audience questions that haven't been asked due to time constraints, and we send them to our guests and we continue the dialogue in that way. So, the remaining questions will be addressed. I want to thank our guests.

Lastly, I want to say that humility is one of the most needed and desirous of virtues, and ego is probably one of the most dangerous of delusions. One of the reasons I chose these four people is because I know in their lives they do make that free will decision to act. They may actually have been a little too humble because they are not only people who can share thoughts with us, they are also examples for all of us. So I really want to thank you all for being here. Thank you for coming. It is an academic institution, but we hopefully are trying to go beyond understanding to change things in the short time, as Connie said, that we're here. Thank you very much and thank you for participating.

APPENDIX 1

Participant Biographies (current at the time of the Interactive Dialogue)

JOHN GRAYZEL (Moderator) assumed the Baháʾí Chair for World Peace professorship in January 2006. He is a former U.S. Senior Foreign Service and USAID (U.S. Agency for International Development) mission director to the Democratic Republic of the Congo. During his almost three decades in government, Professor Grayzel served in Africa, Asia, and the Middle East and as an official representative to various international organizations.

PATRICK CRONIN, Director of the National Defense University's Institute for National Strategic Studies, Senior Advisor and Senior Director of the Asia Program, Center for a New American Century, former U.S. Agency for International Development (USAID) Assistant Administrator for Policy and Program Coordination, and former Director of Research at the U.S. Institute of Peace.

KISHAN MANOCHA, Secretary-General of the national governing council of the Baháʾí community in the United Kingdom, Fellow of the Montreal Institute for Genocide and Human Rights Studies, former lawyer and psychiatrist.

MISHKAT AL-MOUMIN, Adjunct Professor of Environmental Science at George Mason University, former Educational Consultant to the United States Institute of Peace, former Minister of Environment in the Iraqi Interim Government.

CONSTANCE NEWMAN, Special Counsel for African Affairs at the Carmen Group, former United States Assistant Secretary of State for African Affairs, and former USAID Assistant Administrator for Africa.

APPENDIX 2

Audience Questions

Editor's note: Reproduced below are all of the questions submitted—in writing—by audience members during the second Interactive Dialogue. Due to time constraints, it was not possible to pose and answer all questions during the proceedings. Questions are listed here in the approximate order in which they were submitted. Finally, most questions were handed in unsigned (names that were included have been removed here).

Is it possible to attain real human security within the framework of national sovereignty as understood today?

෴

What do you think is the greatest source of insecurity in today's world?

෴

Power structures, in government and economics, are hierarchical in nature, which results in inherent injustices. What is the best way for non-violent advocates to reverse these injustices while respecting the autonomy of governments worldwide?

෴

How important or beneficial might communication technologies become in the advancement of human security and, conversely, how much danger is posed to human security by their misuse?

෴

What can an average college student do to promote a more peaceful, non-militaristic policy on human security? And don't say "vote" because that is a cop-out.

෴

Globalization is a pervasive force that has fundamentally altered our daily interactions. For better or worse, how has globalization changed the nature of human security for the developing world?

◈

What revolutionary actions or movements are occurring today that may actually be considered as promoting peace—and of course human security—not only in the short-term but also in the long term? To what extent are these revolutions motivated by individuals, small or large groups? How sustainable are they and how applicable are they to other locales in the world?

◈

For Dr. Al Moumin:
You argue basic needs of civilians should be met before providing security. How do you stop resource distribution from supplying an insurgency? What's Dr. Cronin's view, particularly coming from CNAS?

◈

What role do, or can, truth and reconciliation commissions play in post-conflict areas of the Islamic World to ensure human security?

◈

I feel that there are always brilliant solutions to security problems when people motivated by peace get together to figure out solutions. But it seems like these non-violent solutions never make it to the ears of the military strategists who realistically have the big power in many of these situations. How can these insightful solutions be more regularly utilized by mainstream security strategists?

◈

Is there a difference between religious and non-religious people and how they deal with human security matters?

◈

How is that human capacity building on the grassroots level can ensure human security worldwide?

꒱

Given the argument for public goods in a "human secure" world, what is the role of the international community in intervening when a state cannot provide them?

꒱

Justice—we have not talked about justice. And especially these days, justice in pursuit of perpetrators of war crimes, crimes against humanity and genocide. It is very exciting to see the U.S., under President Obama, get more involved in the ICC [International Criminal Court]. Why can't/won't we give more teeth to the ICC?

꒱

How does international human migration, i.e. refugees, or even Internally Displaced People, fit into the human security model—in terms of balancing human responsibility to each other with more practical concerns about resource allocation and potential conflicts?

꒱

Why, after much proof of the benefit of making decisions with global best interest in mind, does the U.S. continue to act with solely its own isolated interest in mind?

꒱

How do power relations play out in American security policy?

꒱

When it comes down to it will world governments actually act on these impending issues—namely global warming, AIDS, and energy matters?

꒱

How can we, as citizens, really get the point across that it's time to act, that we've talked and circled around the issue enough?

❧

What is your opinion re: the role of education or lack thereof in creating and sustaining national security and thus world security (i.e., compulsory education literacy without regard to gender or ethnicity).

❧

What is the biggest barrier to nations working together in order to improve the security of developing nations and how is the leading approach to breaking this barrier fairing today, and how should it evolve?

❧

For Patrick Cronin: Does our government's secularity help or hinder our government's ability to get "it," and how?

❧

What kind of a role do/should local communities have in providing security for their citizens & addressing an issue such as piracy?

❧

How can local communities be empowered to have more of a role from the bottom up in providing security?

❧

For Kishan Manocha:
Is global peace possible without having peaceful hearts? If not, how do we teach leaders and children to have peaceful hearts?

❧

I am only one person, what do I do?

❧

Which comes first, peace or economic development?

༃

After the fall of Communism, the U.S. believed its own propaganda; capitalism was the correct path to prosperity and happiness. We have been exporting this way of materialism to every country under the flag of democracy, creating as a consequence, greed, frustration and anxiety. Please comment.

༃

"Education" and "Awareness" always seem to be potential solutions, so how do American educators teach human security in an effective way in such an individualistic society?

༃

Can the world ever experience peace if the West does not fully acknowledge its role and seek forgiveness from the so-called developing world for its centuries of inhumanity in the Third World which had grown deep seeds of distrust and chaos, e.g. Democratic Republic of Congo?

༃

What is the role of cooperation in dealing with the place of religion and religious values by religious and non-religious people in dealing with human security matters?

༃

Bahá'u'lláh (the prophet & founder of the Bahá'í Faith) stated that, "The essence of true safety is to look to the ends of things and renounce the world". Perhaps human security involves more of a "big picture" view of goals for all human security in the world formed through unity between different governmental systems rather than confined to individual nations' preoccupations. What are any of your views on this?

༃

1. How do you define how a nation "feels?" You mentioned that nations feel insecure vs. secure, how is this measured/conceived?

2. How do you define Universal Spiritual values? The term "Spiritual" is a little tricky, it implies religion, and as Constance [Newman] mentioned, dangerous. Is there even such thing as universal values? It seems almost against human security to enforce culture change, even if it is under the term "ethics" & "values".

ళ

The greatest threat to human security is the "war system" (the institution of war), including the obscene amount of money, talent and human resources spent on war. However, in the meantime, it seems people all over the world are getting tired of war. Millions of people marched for peace even before the U.S. invaded Iraq in 2003. Public opinion polls show the American people are becoming more peace-oriented and against foreign interventions. Do you think we can end war in our lifetime?

ళ

To what degree are disparities in education, economic opportunities and other social determinants of health responsible for the lack of collective security?

ళ

Is it possible to create consent to a secular global governance under one political ideology or is it more realistic to build global tolerance and cooperation between separate beliefs and ideologies?

ళ

What can we, as individuals, offer to advance the concept, the progress and the reality of human security?

ళ

Kishan Manocha touched on the need to incorporate spiritual, transcendental values into our approach to dealing with human security. However, many Western governments determinately reject the role of religion in policy-making and foreign relations. How does he (or anyone) propose to infuse religious values into secular governments?

༰

What principles and beliefs do nations need to have to be able to bring human security into policy? Why is the U.S., a supposed great, leading nation, so far behind other nations in being able to have human security as a priority?

༰

Security of a human comes from the security of the society they live in. Security is the trusting confidence of the people in the just living environment no matter how diverse created by the government or may be provided by the other leaders such as religions, social, intellectual, and so on. What is the role of these leaders in helping to provide security in any societies (political leaders are not full-heartedly respected and supported by members of societies)? Power is usually in the hands of governments, where do governments and real, respected leaders of peoples meet and work towards the security of societies?

༰

Concerted action necessitates unity of vision. United under the ideals of compassion, genuine concern for the wellbeing of others, hope for a more harmonious future, etc. Human security can be worked toward through the empowerment of people. A framework for spiritual and social empowerment exists in the core activities of the Bahá'í Faith (community devotional gatherings, children's virtue classes, study circles on spiritual themes, and most importantly the junior youth empowerment program). How can this framework emerge from the private sphere and into public life while addressing concerns for the uncertainty of religion's position in the society along with the supposed imposition of a particular moral code/set of religious ethics?

༰

Security: The UNCHS defines human security as the protection and enhancement of human freedoms and fulfillment. In places of this planet, where there is the greatest security and freedom we find an increase in irresponsible human behavior leading to significant transmission of lethal STDs and obesity leading to unnecessary morbidity and mortality. If security is to protect "fundamental freedoms" does it come without people moderating behavior in a more responsible manner in exchange for the freedom gained?

☞

For some reason, many people assume that the solution to conflict is military might in order to bring about security. However, leaders like Oscar Arias and Muhammad Yunnus have shown the power of non-violent strategies to bring security. Why isn't peaceful intervention currently discussed with the same legitimacy as military intervention? And what needs to be done to bring non-violent intervention the forefront of strategies to bring about security?

☞

What role does the media have in invoking a feeling of security/insecurity for the population? How has this role changed with easy access to the Internet and its use as a means of distributing information?

☞

One way to suggest increased human security at the individual, local, and national levels is to turn "having/holding" into "sharing," and "commanding" into "service." How do we do that at the individual, local, and national levels?

☞

Security [can be defined as]:
• Right not to be oppressed by my own government and military
• Right not to be oppressed by other groups within my country
• Right & opportunity to work and gain a living
• Right to basic services, shelter, water, food, peace etc.
• Right to get education
• Right to hear truth from my leaders

APPENDIX 3

Response to Audience Questions by John Grayzel

The written questions submitted by audience members (see Appendix 2) constituted an integral part of the "dialogue" process as envisioned by the event's organizers. Audience questions are, indeed, the very element that makes the Interactive Dialogue truly *interactive*. They introduce new considerations, represent a check on the ideas stated by the panel, and provide a vital aspect so often missing in many public lectures: allowing presenters to obtain a sense of how their thoughts have been heard. In short, audience questions, especially when submitted in writing, allow speakers to revisit their statements in light of how others have understood them.

Having served as Moderator of the Interactive Dialogue summarized in this publication, I have taken responsibility to produce a "synthesized" response to the audience questions. I have tried to draw accurately on the opinions expressed by the panelists, both during the dialogue and afterwards in further discussions with me on these questions. To their thoughts I have certainly added my own, but at all times I have tried to be as true as possible to each discussant's—and each questioner's—expressed position on human security. The essence of this exercise is to delve into the promises and challenges raised by human security as the international community contemplates adopting it as a major global doctrine.

～

It seems reasonable to begin with a core question asked by several people during the Dialogue: is it possible to attain genuine human security within the framework of national sovereignty, as that concept is understood today?

In response, evidence demonstrates that there is presently no truly shared and commonly practiced framework for national sovereignty—let alone for the concept of human security. Inconsistencies exist not only between, but also within, countries.

Examining the experience of the U.S. reveals the elastic nature of sovereignty today. The United States has been among the most prominent defenders of national sovereignty, and this attitude has played a major role in the American domestic debate over membership in international organizations such as the UN; similarly, concern over sovereignty has led the United State to reject ratification of key international agreements. The U.S., for example, is the only nation, other than Somalia, that has not accepted the UN Convention on the Rights of Children. Political conservatives, who argue that the convention impinges on U.S. sovereignty, have mounted major opposition to it. Yet the United States played a central role in drafting the document, and many of the ideas it expresses actually originate in the U.S. Constitution.

Conversely, in response to (real or perceived) security threats, the United States has repeatedly, both militarily and diplomatically, impinged on the sovereignty of other countries (think of Panama, Iraq, Afghanistan, Chile, and Hawaii, just to cite a few cases). As Dr. Cronin says, "the world is both working on this global-transnational set of trends in human security and it's also still very much mired in nineteenth century, balance-of-power politics. Both are co-existing."

The case can be made that, although a "start and stop" process leading to human security exists, obtaining meaningful and enduring progress in this field will only happen when the most powerful countries agree on a new, twenty-first century global principle of "limited sovereignty." Until that happens, there will be inconsistencies and increasingly tense contradictions in both the international and domestic behaviors of the major world powers. For example, the United States has not only failed to ratify the UN Convention on the Rights of Children—an international issue—but, domestically, its own justice system displays a myriad of inconsistencies with respect to the treatment of both minors and adults.

Inconsistencies in the positions and practices of the United States are pertinent because no deep discussion of human security and its viability as a doctrine can take place without addressing the vital issue of justice. How the leaders and peoples of the world understand and act on their feelings and thoughts about justice is at the core of their attitudes to both sovereignty and human security.

One Dialogue questioner writes: "Power structures, in government and economics, are hierarchical in nature, which results in inherent injustices. What is the best way for non-violent advocates to reverse these injustices while respecting the autonomy of governments worldwide?" Another observes, "It is very exciting to see the U.S., under President Obama, get more involved in the ICC [International Criminal Court]. [But] why can't/won't we give more teeth to the ICC?"

On the question of justice Dr. Cronin pragmatically notes, "there is no way to eradicate injustice, but we can reduce the space for injustice. We can create checks and balances, political processes. We can build institutions, globally and in terms of civil society, to help check this." At the same time he states that it is not just a matter of pragmatics but that "[w]e have to be willing to live for something larger than ourselves and try to find ways to create justice and human security in our own communities."

If we wish to align these thoughts on justice, perhaps we can do so by looking directly at our own lives, families, and communities and asking how we can remediate those injustices we find at our own feet. Both logic and pragmatics suggest that it is only by building *local* foundations for justice through *local* actions that we will construct a sold basis for national and international principles of justice and the measures that flow from them.

Such an approach would address several other audience questions, such as: "What kind of a role do/should local communities have in providing security for their citizens…?" and "How can local communities be empowered to have more of a role from the bottom up in providing security?"

Dr. Al-Moumin expresses her belief that "the grassroots level movement always starts by reaching out to people who think like us or have the same values or acknowledge the same principle, and then the movement grows and grows until it becomes a force for change." At the same time, she draws on her experience in Iraq when she says, "[h]uman security is about meeting basic needs. If you don't meet them, you are going to face political instability and insurgency." On the surface, these two statements may seem contradictory in that one stresses *people and personal relations* and the other *material goods and services*. But in fact, they are integrated in everyday life. Thus, Dr. Al-Moumin recalls how, in Iraq, the failure of the U.S. and its Iraqi partners to meet the basic needs of the population forced Iraqi communities to turn to the available alternatives, including cooperation with radical, anti-American forces.

Many of the questions submitted during the Dialogue build on the phenomenon of human choice by asking, in different ways, what motivates people to act or not act and how we can differentiate between "legitimate" and "illegitimate" acts? One questioner inquires: "Given the argument for public goods in a 'human secure' world, what is the role of the international community in intervening when a state cannot provide them?" Someone else queries: "Why, after much proof of the benefit of making decisions with global best interest in mind, does the U.S. continue to act with solely its own isolated interest in mind?"

One questioner implies that self-protection is the key to explaining behavior: "You argue basic needs of civilians should be met before providing security. [But] how do you stop resource distribution from supplying an insurgency?" Another, however, focuses on the failure of leadership, or the processes in place, when they state: "I feel that there are always brilliant solutions to security problems when people motivated by peace get together to figure out solutions. But it seems like these non-violent solutions never make it to the ears of the military strategists who realistically have the big power in many of these situations. How can these insightful solutions be more regularly utilized by mainstream security strategists?"

Connie Newman offers insight from her professional experience into a seeming contradiction between good decision-making processes and the actual decisions leaders make. In reflecting on differing approaches to human security, she proposes a three-facet model: "... there are countries that get it and do it. There are countries that get it, but don't do it. And there are countries that don't have a clue....in the first group, I put Botswana...they've integrated human security into their whole approach to security of the nation. Ethiopia, on the other hand, gets it but doesn't do it...it's not in the government's interest...[A third position is held by] the Democratic Republic of the Congo, and it doesn't have a clue...the leadership there has not had the time, the interest, or the resources to deal with human security and doesn't even try to talk about it."

Building upon this observation and using it as an exercise in reflection, we can utilize Newman's typology to clarify the positions and actions of other individuals, groups, organizations, and countries, including the United States.

The category of "getting it," for example, is incorporated in the question: "For some reason, many people assume that the solution to conflict is (using) military-might in order to bring about security. However, leaders like Oscar Arias and Muhammad Yunnus have shown the power of non-violent strategies to bring security. Why isn't peaceful intervention currently discussed with the same legitimacy as military intervention?"

The example of a "get it but don't do it" approach is found in the observation/question: "The greatest threat to human security is the 'war system', including the obscene amount of money, talent and human resources spent on war. However, in the meantime, it seems people all over the world are getting tired of war. Millions of people marched for peace even before the U.S. invaded Iraq in 2003. Public opinion polls show the American people are becoming more peace-oriented and against foreign interventions. Do you think we can end war in our lifetime?"

Lastly, an example of "doesn't have a clue" is implied in the query: "After the fall of Communism, the U.S. believed its own propaganda; capitalism was the correct path to prosperity and happiness. We have been exporting this way of materialism to every country under the flag of democracy, creating as a consequence, greed, frustration and anxiety."

To these converging questions, Dr. Manocha sees an underlying commonality when he replies: "[When] it comes to individuals, they have to want change; they have to have a compelling vision of what they can do, the way the world could be; the way society should be; they have to own it at a very, very deep level—it's not at an intellectual level—it has to be at a level that touches their spirit, their core, their being; and then they have to do it." Dr. Manocha's emphasis on what he sees as the essential need to touch the spiritual core of each human explicitly extends the issues that must be addressed under the human security approach.

Many of the issues and answers addressed during the Dialogue, such as the preceding observation, relate to one of the "messiest" aspects of human security: how does one navigate—conceptually and operationally—between *individual* suffering and *national* responsibilities, especially when so many concerns and suggested responses are couched as human phenomenon? This anthropomorphizing of institutions, such as when people speak of "corporate conscience" or "responsible governance," invites confusion as to who is acting and who is even capable of doing so. The challenge goes beyond semantics in that such anthropomorphic understandings are actually embedded in law, for example in the American legal system's extension of constitutional rights to corporations. In this vein, another questioner asks: "How do you define how a nation 'feels?' You mentioned that nations feel insecure vs. secure. How is this measured/conceived?"

To this, Dr. Manocha suggests that feelings are always individual, but individual feelings can be pooled to create larger social and societal realities, thus transforming feelings into social action: "When you identify fundamental principles in life which lead to practical solutions, then you have the beginnings of a sustainable process and you build into that other ways of reflecting on your experiences and you move along in that direction. But at some stage a person has to really want to allow themselves to be influenced to be a source of good, of change, and an agent for promoting the very best of civilization."

If one accepts Dr. Manocha's reliance on the development of personal principles, then from a pragmatic perspective one is lead to ask, "From where do such principles come and how can they be effected?" Moreover, within the context of larger constructs, such as "human security" or "global governance" or "universal rights and responsibility," foundational principles are not just personal expressions of belief. It is at the nexus of individual understanding and larger, shared understandings within frameworks such as "civilization," "society," and "the nation," that the importance of principles is socially constructed and expressed.

The idea of a world of behavior built on fundamental or foundational principles prompts inquiry into the basis of such principles. Is it, as a questioner asks, "…the role of education…[even more specifically]… compulsory education…without regard to gender or ethnicity?" Is it religion, as another inquires: "Is there a difference between religious and non-religious people and how they deal with human security matters?" Can one avoid fighting (over different principles) through "cooperation," as an inquirer implies by asking: "What is the role of cooperation in dealing with the place of religion and religious values by religious and non-religious people in dealing with human security matters?"

Connie Newman discusses the individual origin of such principles; they are, she says, something we must be taught to understand in our early life. "Each of us," she asserts, "has an obligation to pass on—whether it's to a child, grandchild, or whether it's a teacher to a student—the lessons, (and) the values that are necessary to make society work in a fair way. I vaguely remember my parents…saying to me, 'First of all, life is short. It's not totally fair. You have an obligation to give back.'"

Who enjoys the authority or legitimacy to determine what should be an established group principle or an accepted individual obligation? Is it our parents, our teachers, religion, political correctness, etc.? In the end, the specifics of an individual's foundational principles may vary, but at the same time we can find a commonality in the existence of a shared acceptance of the need for foundational principles per se.

Patrick Cronin expresses his belief that: "[W]e all have to have a philosophy of life that, hopefully, is larger than ourselves, and an understanding that we have a responsibility to protect the rights of others and their freedoms." Such "larger philosophies of life" are, of course, critical determinants of meaning in our lives and, as such, they can be powerful drivers of our sense of individual dignity. This aspect of higher meaning and understanding relates directly to on-the-ground human security concerns in that the opportunity to have dignity, and to afford or deny someone else respect, is a significant aspect of physical and spiritual security. Dr. Manocha emphasizes how "…there is the entire body of humanity's religious experience to draw on…that entire body of values, of insight into human nature, into what truly motivates the human being and gives shape and fullness to the human life. … Those principles are there to be drawn on and to be examined and applied…with science…these two great sources of knowledge…."

If we grant that principles exist and are a proper basis for action, then the need arises to provide meaningful answers to questions such as these, which were posed during the Dialogue: "What can an average college student do to promote a more peaceful, non-militaristic policy on human security?" And, "I am only one person, what do I do?" And also, "What can we, as individuals, offer to advance the concept, the progress and the reality of human security?"

Dr. Al-Moumin suggests that a place to begin is the way one works with others: "You empower the people to meet their needs. You don't do it for them. You empower them, build their capacity so they can do it themselves." At the same time there exists a conundrum at the heart of calls for, and claims of, empowering others in that these imply that the person to be empowered is dependent on another to become empowered. This phenomenon often plays out in daily life when teenagers reject adult authority precisely because they wish to assert their independence. An analogous scenario influences international development. "Weaker" nations often refuse or divert foreign assistance that is looked upon as compromising their immediate authority—such as refusing to comply with standards of international commercial contracting—even when such assistance would help them become more respected and powerful.

Perhaps human security needs to be examined not just as a problem to be solved, but also as an alternative, proactive avenue for achieving greater equity in a globalized world. Dr. Cronin notes that despite the problems arising from globalization, the phenomenon has conferred immense potential power on groups and individuals. He also observes that the diffusion of technologies "cuts both ways. [With] communication technology for social mobilization...everybody in this room has the capacity to mobilize other people in a way we've never had before through communication."

If there is truth to the preceding observations, then achieving human security may be even more closely tied to *individual* action than it is to state or international action. Likewise, the failure to achieve human security may be ascribed, primarily, to lack of individual action. Dr. Manocha notes that problems often arise because we become mired in doubt rather than moving to action. Drawing on his experience as a psychiatrist, he observes, "I think one of the things that individuals do well is they know what needs to be done. They know, for example—if they're seeing a psychiatrist or psychotherapist—that the way to live a better life is to block out the negative thoughts. Where they don't do so well is the actually blocking out the negative thoughts. You sit there and they come back to you week in and week out with the same old negative assumptions about themselves, the way the world is, and how powerless they are. And you say, 'Now do it; just do it.' There has to be a recognition somewhere within them that now is the time to do it. Walk that path and see how far you get and see what life is like on the other side."

Such counsel, of course, raises the need for even more guidance. In this regard, Connie Newman shares this wisdom: "Everybody in this room knows of a place where they can serve. Everybody could take one brick and add it to another brick that already exists and make a difference. What is often the problem is …we're looking for that one place where we're going to see a major change but change comes incrementally."

If we place the reflections of Dr. Manocha and Ms. Newman together, then we are prompted to consider the very originating basis of our motivations. Posed as a question, "How does one become motivated to take the first step?" The Founding Fathers of the Untied States often spoke about the need to create "a Republic of Virtues." In this context, virtues can be understood as values embedded in repeated behaviors. It is said that George Washington carried a list of virtues in his pocket as a constant reminder to guide his behavior. Perhaps relevant to the question of values and virtues is Dr. Manocha's assertion that there is "…one practical thing that anyone can really do, and that is to understand that value—the oneness of humanity—and to align oneself with that value. But most of all, teach it to the young people."

For Dr. Al-Moumin, maximizing values involves not just teaching them but also dialoguing on them as widely as possible: "Spread the word about it. Tell people about it. You can go on Facebook and ask a question about it. You can go on Twitter and tweet about it. You can reach out to the next-do≠or neighbor and see if she or he thinks like you."

In this regard, however, it is critical to avoid naivety and its attendant dangers. All the powerful tools of modern communications can be used for nefarious as well as laudable purposes. Communications wars can be, in their own way, as dangerous as traditional military conflicts. The genocide in Rwanda was perpetrated, in part, through widespread use of "hate radio" by the killers.

Dr. Cronin reflects on how the career of Roméo Dallaire, the former commander of UN forces in Rwanda during the 1994 crisis, can serve as both a model and caution of global citizenship: "After the genocide, Roméo Dallaire had a nervous breakdown. He slept on benches; he was a broken man. So there are a couple of lessons from that. One of them is simply that as you get involved in these issues, they are not hazard-free. …[action] is going to create winners and losers, it's also going to shake you….From his experience, he got off that bench. He wrote a book. He has become a force for good. He has helped to mobilize a great deal of political action to help prevent genocide in the future."

So where does this leave us? Every one of us cannot be a George Washington or a Roméo Dallaire. The panel's clear message, however, is that there is a place for all and that "great" and "small" are relative measures that change over time. Everyone can do *something* now to advance human security, both their own and that of others. Connie Newman explains how great changes can begin with incremental measures: "What I'm saying to the students is that they can look out their window…and see a place to make a small difference—if their attitude is that they're satisfied with …[what is available to do] for the time being, because it will lead [in the future] to their ability to make larger differences."

Looking back on the Dialogue and the thoughts and responses our discussion provoked, it seems clear that whether or not the concept of human security is an official doctrine for a particular government or international organization, "human security" resides at the heart of not only what humans *need*, but also what humans *are*. Human security is—but is not only—about material wellbeing. It is also about how we see the spiritual meaning of life and our understood purpose in possessing life and how we live it.

Human security is fundamentally about the actions we take, in relation to each other, based on a purposeful sense of responsibility to do what we believe is right, each according to our principles exercised in accord with our given capacities.

APPENDIX 4

Some Representations of Human Security (Various Figures)

Figure 1: Theories of International Relations

Editor's note: The chart reproduced below can be thought of as presenting a "classic" range of International Relations theories, none of which explicitly incorporates the human security approach. The Global-Humanist perspective, however, does include elements such as "equal opportunity" and "basic needs" that closely align with the concept of human security.

	Realist	Corporate-Globalist	Global Humanist
Institutional	Bargaining	Access	Accountability
	Influence	Hierarchy	Democratic management
	Mission	Influence	Equal opportunity
	Control	Consumption	Decentralization
Norms	Alliance system	Capitalism	Basic needs
	Hegemony	Global culture	Interdependence
	National mission	Interdependence	International retimes
	Protectionism	Laissez-faire	'One world'
	Intervention	Integration	International law
Structure	System-maintaining	System-maintaining	System-transforming
	Power blocs	Liberal order	World order

Source:
Mel Gurtov, *Global Politics in the Human Interest* (Boulder, CO: Lynne Rienner, 1999), 25-26.

Figure 2: Realms of human security

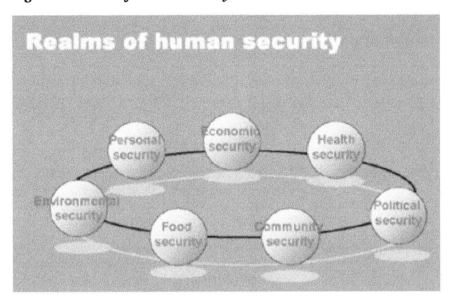

Source:

Jan Van Dijk, "Human Security: A New Agenda For Integrated, Global Action," keynote lecture at the International Conference on Space and Water: Towards Sustainable Development and Human Security, Santiago de Chile, Chile, 1-2 April, 2004 (available from [http://www.unodc.org/unodc/en/ about-unodc/speeches/speech_2004-04-01_1.html]; accessed 18 September 2009). At the time of this lecture, the author was Officer in Charge, Human Security Branch, Division of Operations, United Nations Office of Drugs and Crime, Vienna.

Figure 3: Seven dimensions of human security

Economic security	Assured basic income: access to employment and resources.
Food security	Physical and economic access to food for all people at all times. Hundreds of millions of people in the world remain hungry either through local unavailability of food or, more often, through lack of entitlements or resources to purchase food.
Health security	Access to medical treatment and improved health conditions. Poor people in general have less health security and in developing countries, the major causes of death are infectious and parasitic diseases.
Environmental security	Living in a healthy physical environment which is spared form desertification, deforestation and other environmental threats that endanger people's survival.
Personal security	Individual security from physical violence. Threats can take several forms, for example: threats from the State, foreign states, other groups of people (ethnic tension), individuals or gangs; threats directed against women or children based on their vulnerability and dependence; threats to self (e.g. suicide, drug use, etc.).
Community security	Most people derive their security from membership of a social group (family, community, organization, political grouping, ethnic grouping, etc.). Tensions often arise between these groups due to competition over limited access to opportunities and resources.
Political security	Living in a society that guarantees basic human rights and freedom of expression.

Source:
Karim Hussein, Donata Gnisci and Julia Wanjiru, *Security and Human Security: An Overview of Concepts and Initiatives—What Implications for West Africa?* (Paris: Sahel and West Africa Club, 2004), 13, summarizing the findings contained in United Nations Development Programme, *Human Development Report 1994* (New York: Oxford University Press, 1994).

Figure 4: Human security

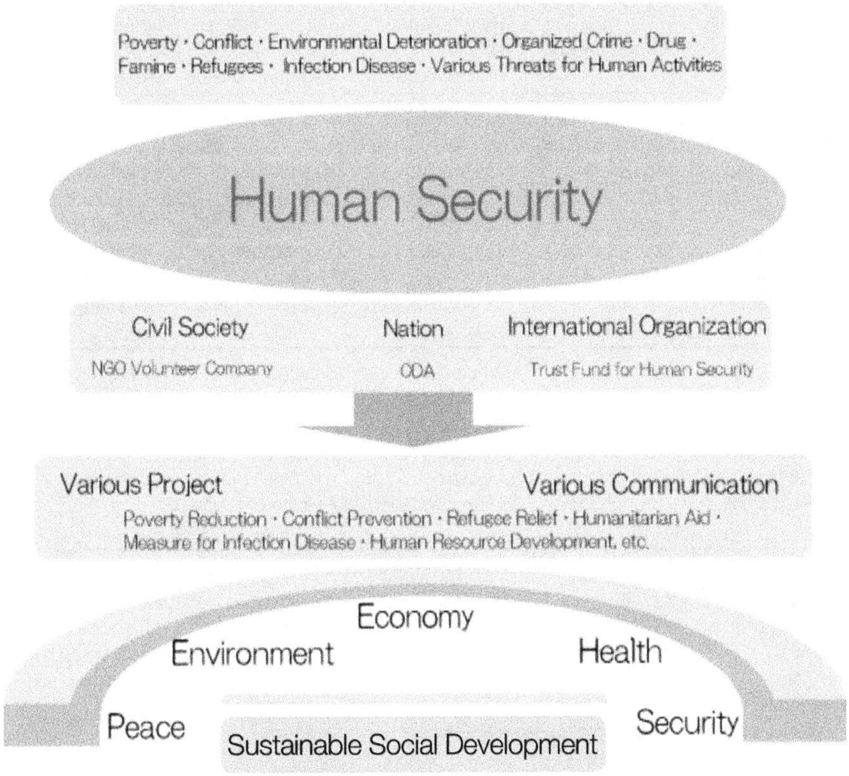

Poverty · Conflict · Environmental Deterioration · Organized Crime · Drug · Famine · Refugees · Infection Disease · Various Threats for Human Activities

Human Security

| Civil Society | Nation | International Organization |
| NGO Volunteer Company | ODA | Trust Fund for Human Security |

Various Project   Various Communication

Poverty Reduction · Conflict Prevention · Refugee Relief · Humanitarian Aid · Measure for Infection Disease · Human Resource Development, etc.

Economy

Environment   Health

Peace   Sustainable Social Development   Security

Source:
Graduate Program on Human Security, University of Tokyo (available from [http://human-security.c.u-tokyo.ac.jp/eng/]; accessed 16 September 2009).

Figure 5: Key human security clusters following violent conflict

Public safety	Humanitarian relief	Rehabilitation and reconstruction	Reconciliation and coexistence	Governance and empowerment
Control armed elements • Enforce cease-fire • Disarm combatants • Demobilize combatants	Facilitate return of conflict-affected people • Internally displaced persons • Refugees	Integrate conflict-affected people • Internally displaced persons • Refugees • Armed combatants	End impurity • Set up tribunals • Involve traditional justice processes	Establish rule of law framework • Institute constitution, judicial system, legal reform • Adapt legislation • Promote human rights
Protect civilians • Establish law and order, fight criminal violence • Clear landmines • Collect small arms	Assure food security • Meet nutrition standards • Launch food production	Rehabilitate infrastructure • Roads • Housing • Power • Transportation	Establish truth • Set up truth commission • Promote forgiveness • Restore dignity of victims	Initiate political reform • Institutions • Democratic processes
Build national security institutions • Police • Military • Integrate/dissolve non-state armed elements	Ensure health security • Provide access to basic health care • Prevent spread of infectious diseases • Provide trauma and mental health care	Promote social protection • Employment • Food • Health • Education • Shelter	Announce amnesties • Immunity from prosecution for lesser crimes • Reparation for victims	Strengthen civil society • Participation • Accountability • Capacity building
Protect external security • Combat illegal weapons and drugs trade • Combat trafficking in people • Control borders	Establish emergency safety net for people at risk • Women (female-headed households); children (soldiers); elderly; indigenous people; missing people	Dismantle war economy • Fight criminal networks • Re-establish market economy • Provide micro-credit	Promote coexistence • Encourage community-based initiatives (long-term) • Rebuild social capital	Promote access to information • Independent media • Transparency

Source:
Commission on Human Security, *Human Security Now* (New York: Commission on Human Security, 2003), 60.

Figure 6: Regional vs. international intervention as a prelude to human security

Regional intervention	International intervention
Advantages	**Disadvantages**
→ Local actors: action informed by local knowledge. Strong interest in ending the conflict → Political will to end the conflict to avoid its consequences on neighboring countries → More rapid deployment of forces on the ground → Expensive for African countries, but relatively cheap compared to UN missions → Way to enhance African capacity to respond to internal problems	→ External actors: not familiar with local settings → Relatively indifferent: moral motivation to end conflict or economic/strategic interests in the zone → Slow decision-making process → Expensive: international community needed to cover costs → Dependence: influence of former colonial powers remains strong; dependence on long decision-making processes for external aid
Disadvantages	**Advantages**
→ Risk of partiality: vested interests of neighboring countries in the conflict, risks of hegemonic influence by a dominant regional actor → Institutional weaknesses of regional organizations → Lack of logistical capacities and financial resources to sustainably bear the cost of intervention	→ Neutrality: multinational mixed military and civilian personnel less likely to have a stake in the conflict → Strong peacekeeping capacities based on practical international experience (e.g. NATO) → Well equipped, well trained forces

Source:
Karim Hussein, Donata Gnisci and Julia Wanjiru, *Security and Human Security: An Overview of Concepts and Initiatives—What Implications for West Africa?* (Paris: Sahel and West Africa Club, 2004), 24.

Figure 7: Health and human security linkages

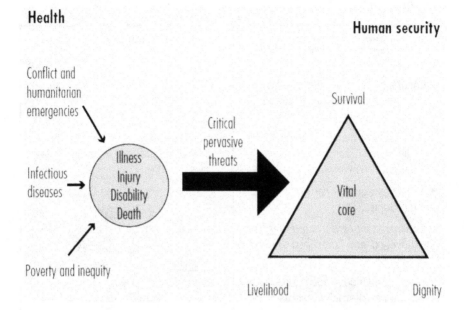

Source:
Commission on Human Security, *Human Security Now* (New York: Commission on Human Security, 2003), 97.

Figure 8: Expanded concepts of "security"

		Mode of expansion		
Degree of expansion	Label	Security of whom? Focus	Security of what? Value at risk	Security from whom or what? Source(s) of threat
No expansion	National security	The state	Sovereignty Territorial integrity	Other states (Sub-state actors)
Incremental	Social security	Nations Societal groups	National unity Indemnity	(States) Nations Migrants Asial culture
Radical	Human security	Individuals Humanity	Survival Quality of life	The state Globalization Nature
Ultra-radical	Environmental security	Ecosystem	Sustainability	Humanity

Source:
Bjørn Møller, "National, Societal and Human Security: General Discussion with a Case Study from the Balkans," in *What Agenda for Human Security in the Twenty-first Century?*, 2d ed., proceedings of the First International Meeting of Directors of Peace Research and Training Institutions convened on 27-28 November 2000 (Paris: UNESCO, 2005), 87.

Figure 9: Where human security (HS) meets human development (HD)–threshold and overlap

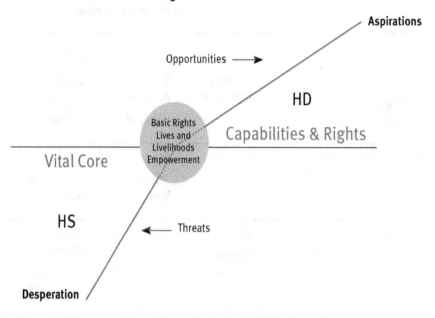

Source:
United Nations Development Programme, *Arab Human Development Report 2009: Challenges to Human Security in the Arab Countries* (New York: United Nations Development Programme, 2009), 20.

Figure 10: The human cost of military spending in developing countries

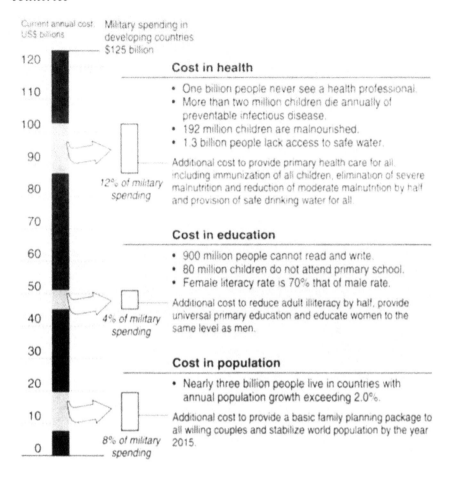

Current annual cost US$ billions

Military spending in developing countries
$125 billion

Cost in health

- One billion people never see a health professional.
- More than two million children die annually of preventable infectious disease.
- 192 million children are malnourished.
- 1.3 billion people lack access to safe water.

12% of military spending

Additional cost to provide primary health care for all, including immunization of all children, elimination of severe malnutrition and reduction of moderate malnutrition by half and provision of safe drinking water for all.

Cost in education

- 900 million people cannot read and write.
- 80 million children do not attend primary school.
- Female literacy rate is 70% that of male rate.

4% of military spending

Additional cost to reduce adult illiteracy by half, provide universal primary education and educate women to the same level as men.

Cost in population

- Nearly three billion people live in countries with annual population growth exceeding 2.0%.

8% of military spending

Additional cost to provide a basic family planning package to all willing couples and stabilize world population by the year 2015.

Source:
United Nations Development Programme, *Human Development Report 1994* (New York: Oxford University Press, 1994), 50.

APPENDIX 5

Human Security and the United States Agency for International Development

Editor's note: The following document was drafted by the Office of Policy Development and Cooperation in the Bureau for Policy and Program Coordination (PDC/PDC) of the United States Agency for International Development (USAID) in December 2000 and revised in January 2001. At that time, Professor John Grayzel (Moderator of the Interactive Dialogue published above) was the PDC/PPC Office Director. The text is reproduced, with minor edits, from a copy in his possession.

The significance of this document resides in the fact that it embodies an official, operational recognition and positive assessment of the potential of "human security" to serve as an over-arching doctrine of international development. Interactive Dialogue discussants repeatedly stated that the U.S. Government disregards the concept and practice of human security; if true, this document indicates that the value of the human security approach was recognized and even proposed as a policy option, though it failed to gain either political or bureaucratic traction.

᧤

Human Security and USAID

Introduction

The prevailing model of sustainable development has suffered significant shocks in the last decade as conflict, economic and political upheavals, increased criminality and disasters presented major reversals in development progress on all continents. International Donor institutions like USAID find themselves facing a dramatically changing development landscape. Increasingly, programs and activities have shifted away from an emphasis on sustainable development to increasing crises responses, whether transition from conflict in Kosovo, to fighting HIV/AIDS, to humanitarian assistance in Central Africa. As a concept, sustainable development embodies the idea of economic and social growth that does not exhaust its resource base. But non-sustainable needs increasingly exhaust foreign assistance resources that are needed for sustainable development.

This note advances the idea that there is a need for a new operational understanding that can incorporate the need to respond to both short-term crisis and long-term stability in complementary and mutually supporting fashions. It suggests that the best candidate to date for such a unifying concept is that of "*human security*."[29] the notion that there are a selected number of needs and interests that motivate and address the needs of the majority of underdeveloped country populations and which, if addressed simultaneously in terms of immediate and long-term solutions, offers a more effective way of structuring most foreign development.

Definition

While definitions vary in scope and complexity, human security embodies the idea of the "universal well being of individuals." In its most modest form it asserts that people should be safe from both violent and non-violent threat. It has also been more broadly defined as assurances of the necessary social, economic, and environmental conditions that affect people's quality of life, whether they have a future, and as "the right of individuals to live, work and participate without fear in the social, political, and economic structures that affect their lives and livelihood." Most of these definitions build upon one in the United Nations 1994 *Human Development Report*, which describes human security as:

> ...the sense that people are free from worries, not merely from the dread of a cataclysmic world event but primarily about daily life. Human security is people-centered while being turned to two different aspects: It means, first, safety from chronic threats of hunger, disease and repression. And second, it means protection from sudden and hurtful disruption in the patterns of daily life—whether in homes, in job or in communities.

Human security is a broad reaching concept that directs our attention away from the development of the nation-state per se to the long-term development, safety, and wellbeing of individuals and communities. It is this encapsulating dimension that has motivated donors like Canada and Japan to embrace human security as the unifying framework of their foreign policy in the 21st century.

---

[29] [Ed.'s note] Emphasis in the original.

How does human security differ from existing frameworks such as "basic needs," "social development," and "poverty?" A "basic needs" approach focuses on fundamental biological and social necessities, i.e., food, water, health and education, as fundamental building blocks of a meaningful life while human security focuses on a wider number of factors: personal security, group security, economic security, environmental security, health security, etc. Human security also accepts that people determine their own priority security interests, based on their real life circumstances (hence the power of properly identified security needs as a motivator for action). Finally, human security sees health, food, and income as elements that are necessary, but differentially weighted, factors in the equations of different lives and circumstances.

A social policy framework "promotes cohesive, stable, just and well functioning societies that respect social, ethnic, and cultural diversities of its members." In one respect, human security defuses the potential volatility of emphasizing social groups. The focus on ensuring that all people are safe and at an adequate level of wellbeing may potentially eliminate the competition between groups often fueled by material and social inequities. It also presupposes that while the security priorities may differ from one social group to another, they all derive from the same basic set of concerns, which can shift depending upon circumstances.

Taking all of these factors into consideration, for the purposes of this note, *we define "Human Security" as the right of individuals and communities to operate with adequate assurance of the opportunity and conditions to have their basic life needs met, to remain free from unjustly inflicted personal harm and injury, to have access to political, economic, and social resources required for meaningful positive social and economic participation, and to live in a reasonable risk-bearable environment.*[30]

As a conceptual policy framework, human security provides a useful paradigm through which international donor agencies such as USAID could begin to better organize current activities in a more coherent fashion, and prepare for the new work that needs to be done. A human security policy integrates social, political, and economic concerns, and combines short-term crisis responses with sustainable development strategies.

Within such a holistic and encapsulating policy strategy, USAID would be able to organize its activities and programs in a more coherent fashion rather than the fragmentary, compartmentalized manner that

---

[30] [Ed.'s note] Emphasis in the original.

reflects an antiquated approach to development assistance. Further, rather than develop different policies to advance the crosscutting themes of gender, civil society, institutional and organizational development, and crisis management, a human security policy would embrace these themes as fundamental components of human security. Through a human security policy, crisis management would be better integrated into longtime Agency programs and activities. Finally, as a framework, human security could accommodate new legislation on Microenterprise for Self-Reliance (PL106-309), the Global AIDS and Tuberculosis Relief Act (PL 106-264), and the Victims of Trafficking and Violence Protection Act (PL 106-386); by focusing work on these areas in contexts where they were real and perceived factors affecting or improving local security interests of the assisted countries and populations.

Background

While human security is definitely an idea whose time has come it is not a new concept. As mentioned earlier, it first appeared in the 1994 United Nations *Human Development Report*. Since that occurrence, a key word search will generate thousands of speeches, reports, articles, books, institutions, and discussions about the relevance of human security in foreign assistance for the 21st century. Some have observed that human security is not "a symbolic concept, but rather a practical necessity that should be used as a tool for bringing about specific action." Others see it as the most important framework to guide foreign assistance in crisis, post-crisis, vulnerable and stable environments that characterize developing countries. Further, the term captures the attention of the developed world by focusing on an issue that is of mutual interest. Everywhere in the world, regardless of status, people are concerned with human security.

USAID and Human Security

Thinking in human security terms is not new to USAID. In February 1995, a draft report entitled "Global Human Security and Sustainable Development" circulated. The report argued that thinking in terms of global human security represented a "new vision of global development." It also noted that "human security is much more than the absence of military threat, it includes security against economic privation [and]...acceptable quality of life, and a guarantee of fundamental human rights." Despite the numerous recommendations made in the report, programs and activities in the Agency continue to operate along more traditional lines. While advocating a human security framework may have been prescient at the time, to ignore it in today's world would be foolish.

Human Security Policy

With the incorporation of cross-cutting themes into the Agency's Strategic Plan, with the increased number of earmarks, and diminishing resources to foreign assistance, new methodologies and frameworks, indeed new policies that serve to direct the Agency's agenda are needed. PPC[31] is in a position, as an objective, non-programmatic bureau to lay the foundation and create a Human Security policy that sets the framework for assessing and organizing the Agency's resources to ensure that sustainable development contributes to global human security.

---

[31] [Ed.'s note] The Bureau for Policy and Program Coordination of USAID.

BIBLIOGRAPHY

Human Security—A Select, Annotated Source List

Note: The Editor compiled and annotated this bibliography.

Commission on Global Governance. *Our Global Neighborhood: The Report of the Commission on Global Governance.* New York: Oxford University Press, 1995.

The independent Commission on Global Governance was established in the early 1990s at the suggestion of Willy Brandt, former chancellor of West Germany (from 1969 to 1974). Brandt personally recruited the Commission's co-chairs, Ingvar Carlsson (of Sweden) and Shridath Ramphal (of Guyana) who, in turn, brought together a twenty-six-member cadre that included international figures like Oscar Arias, Jacques Delors, Sadako Ogata, and Brian Urquhart. In their Foreword to the *Report*, Carlsson and Ramphal state that the Commission is concerned with global *governance* (meaning, among other measures, enhanced international security, trade and law) not global *government* (which could, they warn, lead to more authoritarianism, hegemony, and statism in the world[32]).

Students of "human security" will be most interested in the third chapter of *Our Global Neighborhood*, entitled "Promoting Security." Therein can be found the *Report's* only explicit reference to human security in the form of a passing mention at the conclusion of a brief survey of alternative international security paradigms (also discussed in this section are "common security," "collective security," and "comprehensive security"). Although acknowledging the worthiness of these approaches, the Commission advocates a concept it calls "the security of people and the planet" (pp. xviii, 78, 80, 85, 338). Under this usage, security of the planet means environmental protection on a global scale while security of the people "recognizes that global security extends beyond the protection of borders, ruling elites, and exclusive state interests to

---

[32] The Commission's rejection of global government provoked strong negative reactions among adherents of the "world federalism" movement, several of whose leading lights produced a book entitled *Toward Genuine Global Governance: Critical Reactions to "Our Global Neighborhood"* (Westport, CT: Praeger, 1999).

include the protection of people....[and] must be regarded as a goal as important as the security of states" (p. 81).

Intellectually and functionally human security (as that concept is generally understood) and the security of people are quite similar, if not identical. Significantly, the effectiveness of both is contingent on extending the scope of the UN's mandate beyond the security of states in the international system to include the security of communities and individuals within sovereign borders that are menaced by a range of threats, including any inflicted by their own governments.

⁓

Commission on Human Security. *Human Security Now*. New York: Commission on Human Security, 2003.

Created in 2001 with a two-year lifespan, the independent Commission on Human Security was charged with conceptualizing, publicizing, and operationalizing "human security" as a viable component of international relations. The Commission's major report, *Human Security Now*, provides a comprehensive, if cumbersome,

"...definition of human security: to protect the vital core of all human lives in ways that enhance human freedoms and human fulfilment. Human security means protecting fundamental freedoms—freedoms that are the essence of life. It means protecting people from critical (severe) and pervasive (widespread) threats and situations. It means using processes that build on people's strengths and aspirations. It means creating political, social, environmental, economic, military and cultural systems that together give people the building blocks of survival, livelihood and dignity" (p. 4).

A publication that advocates such an expansive approach might more realistically be called "Human Security *Eventually*." Nevertheless, the task of translating the abstract concept of human security into a real-world action program is somewhat aided by the inclusion of "policy conclusions" at the end of six of the report's eight chapters. The policy recommendations that round out

Chapter 2 ("People Caught Up in Violent Conflict") are typical in that they range from those that depend on an unlikely spontaneous enlightenment ("All actors should recognize the responsibility to rebuild in post-conflict situations") to options that are both innovative and practicable ("The international community should... set up a human security transition fund for each recovery from post-conflict" [p. 33]).

⨍

Craig, Gordon. "The Good Soldier." Review of *George C. Marshall: Statesman, 1945-1959*, by Forrest C. Pogue. *New York Review of Books*, 13 August 1987: 11-13. Reprinted in *Tact and Intelligence: Essays on Diplomatic History and International Relations*, eds. Bruce Thompson, Carolyn Halladay, and Donald Abenheim. Palo Alto, CA: Society for the Promotion of Science and Scholarship, 2008.

"The Good Soldier" reviews the fourth and final volume of Forrest C. Pogue's tetralogy[33] on the life of the American soldier and statesman George Marshall. Historian Gordon Craig opens his assessment of Pogue's work by quoting from a speech General Marshall delivered during the ceremony marking his retirement from the U.S. military, which occurred in November 1945 (just a few months after World War II ended):

"Today this nation with good faith and sincerity, I am certain, desires to take the lead in the measures necessary to avoid another world catastrophe, such as you have just endured. And the world of suffering people looks to us for such leadership. Their thoughts, however, are not concentrated alone on this problem. They have the more immediate and terribly pressing concerns—where the mouthful of food will come from, where they will find shelter tonight and where they will find warmth from the cold of winter. Along with the great problem of maintaining the peace we must solve the problem of the pittance of food, of clothing and coal and

---

[33] The three proceeding volumes in the series are: *George C. Marshall: Education of a General, 1880–1939* (New York: Viking, 1963), *George C. Marshall: Ordeal and Hope, 1939–1943* (New York: Viking, 1966), and *George C. Marshall: Organizer of Victory, 1943–1945* (New York: Viking, 1973). Together, Pogue's four volumes constitute Marshall's "authorized biography" (Marshall himself refused to write his memoirs, even when publishers tried to entice him with lucrative book deals).

homes. Neither of these problems can be solved alone. They are directly related, one to the other" (pp. 269-70).[34]

As Craig notes, the general's words were a prelude to what became known as the Marshall Plan, the initiative by the U.S. Government to stabilize postwar Europe through a coordinated program of economic reconstruction. Marshall's 1945 speech can also be read as a prologue to "human security" in that he directly couples the challenge of maintaining international peace among states with the problem of securing peoples' access to their basic needs. Today, analysts and advocates of human security have similarly underscored this connection.

The military historian Chris Bellamy asserts that studying the Soviet Union's 1941-1945 war effort can illuminate "twenty-first-century security concerns," including "the fine balance to be struck between national security and the human security of the state's inhabitants."[35] In a letter to the editor published in the *New York Times*, Marie Wilson of the White House Project writes that "the globalized world urgently demands a paradigm shift, an integrated approach that treats human security and state security as inseparable and complementary."[36]

In light of the fact that Marshall's Plan continues to enjoy popularity across the American political spectrum—as does his personal record as a military commander—proponents of human

---

[34] In reproducing this quotation, Craig truncates the final sentences thusly: "Along with the great problem of maintaining the peace we must solve [this] problem. . . . Neither of these problems can be solved alone. They are directly related, one to the other." The "missing" text has been reintroduced here based on the epigram that precedes the following essay: J. Bradford De Long and Barry Eichengreen, "The Marshall Plan: History's Most Successful Structural Adjustment Program," paper prepared for the Centre for Economic Performance and Landeszentralbank Hamburg conference on Post-World War II European Reconstruction, Hamburg, September 5-7, 1991 (available from [http://www.j-bradford-delong.net/teaching_Folder/Econ_210a_f99/Readings/Marshall_Large.pdf]; accessed 22 February 2011).

[35] Chris Bellamy, *Absolute War: Soviet Russia in the Second World War* (New York: Alfred A. Knopf, 2007), xxi.

[36] Marie C. Wilson, "Human Security and State Security," letter to the editor, *New York Times*, 3 July 2008 (available from [http://www.nytimes.com/2008/07/03/opinion/lweb03kristof.html]; accessed 3 July 2008).

security could bolster their case by explicitly appealling to the general's thinking on international peace.[37]

ـک

Department of Foreign Affairs and International Trade. "Freedom from Fear: Canada's Foreign Policy for Human Security." Ottawa, Canada: Department of Foreign Affairs and International Trade, 2002.

Because the government of Canada has been a pioneer and leader of the movement to infuse the "human security" approach into international relations, the document "Freedom from Fear" is especially notable and can benefit all those seeking to understand this emerging concept. Admirably succinct at only 16 pages, and featuring an easy-to-digest format, this official statement defines human security as "freedom from pervasive threats to people's rights, safety or lives" (p. 3). In particular, the Canadian government "focusses on increasing people's safety from the threat of violence" (p. 3), an approach that, it says, aligns with the country's established policies in the areas of national security, human rights, and international development.

As described in "Freedom from Fear," Canada advances its human security agenda by concentrating on five priorities: public safety; protection of civilians; conflict prevention; governance and accountability; and peace support operations. Thematically, the report emphasizes the characteristic at the heart of all sustainable human security efforts, namely *partnership* (the last section of "Freedom from Fear" is entitled "Partnerships for human security"). Institutionally, Canada's commitment to human security as a foreign policy priority is demonstrated by its creation of a Human

---

[37] The contention is that Marshall can serve as a posthumous advocate for human security, not that his ideas were original or unique. In June 1945, several months before Marshall delivered his retirement speech, U.S. Secretary of State Edward Stettinius, Jr. declared: "The battle of peace has to be fought on two fronts. The first is the security front where victory spells freedom from fear. The second is the economic and social front where victory spells freedom from want. Only victory on both fronts can assure the world of an enduring peace." Quoted in Hilary French, "Upcoming World Summit Offers Rare Opportunity to Redesign the U.N. for the Future," Worldwatch Global Security Brief #7, 8 September 2005 (available from [www.unep.org/greenroom/documents/WWatch-Brief7-FinalDR.doc]; accessed 28 August 2010).

Security Program (HSP) within its Department of Foreign Affairs and International Trade (DFAIT). Subsequently, the HSP was renamed the Glyn Berry Program for Peace and Security.

For updated information on Canada's human security policies consult the DFAIT's website (www.international.gc.ca/international/index.aspx), especially the webpage of the Glyn Berry Program (www.international.gc.ca/glynberry/index.aspx).

༄

Friends of Human Security. First, second, and third of a continuing series of dialogues on human security held on 19 October 2006, 20 April 2007, and 7 November 2007, respectively (available from [http://www.mofa.go.jp/policy/ human_secu/friends/index.html]; accessed on 15 April 2009).

The "Friends of Human Security" is an unofficial network that periodically holds informal gatherings during which diplomats accredited to the United Nations—together with representatives of international organizations—discuss "human security" and how that concept can guide UN operations. The summaries of these discussions are useful because they clarify key questions about the meaning and significance of human security. During the third meeting of the Friends of Human Security, for example, Mexico's UN representative highlighted an important distinction between human security and the doctrine known as the "responsibility to protect" (often called R2P):

"Ambassador [Claude] Heller emphasized that human security should be understood as a multi-dimensional concept, but should not be considered a synonym for the responsibility to protect. *The responsibility to protect, the representative of Mexico explained, was a reactive concept, while human security lay at the core of a culture of prevention.*"[38]

---

[38] See Co-Chair's Summary, "Third Meeting of Friends of Human Security," held on 7 November 2007 at the United Nations headquarters in New York, (available from [http://www.mofa.go.jp/policy/human_secu/friends/summary0711.html]; accessed 15 April 2009) (emphasis added). In contrast, the scholar Jussi Hanhimäki's seems to treat human security and the responsibility to protect as more or less interchangeable. See Hanhimäki, *The United Nations: A Very Short Introduction* (New York: Oxford University Press, 2008), 126.

Summaries of other Friends of Human Security meetings available online (as of December 2010) include:

• "Fourth Meeting of the Friends of Human Security," 15 May 2008 (available from [http://ochaonline. un.org/OutreachandABHS/Outreach/2008Activities/ FourthMeetingoftheFriendsofHumanSecurity/tabid/4746/ language/en-US/Default.aspx]).

• "Fifth Meeting of the Friends of Human Security," 20 November 2008 (available from [http://ochaonline.un.org/ FifthMeetingoftheFriendsofHumanSecurity/tabid/5529/language/ en-US/Default.aspx]).

• "Sixth Meeting of the Friends of Human Security," 4 June 2009 (available from [http://ochaonline.un.org/ SixthMeetingoftheFriendsofHumanSecurity/tabid/5709/language/ en-US/Default.aspx]).

• "Seventh meeting of Friends of Human Security," 10 December 2009 (available from [http://ochaonline. un.org/OutreachandABHS/Outreach/2009Activities/ SeventhmeetingoftheFriendsofHumanSecurity/tabid/6429/ language/en-US/Default.aspx]).

ॐ

Hanhimäki's, Jussi M. *The United Nations: A Very Short Introduction.* New York: Oxford University Press, 2008.

See note 38 and the bibliography entry below for Siracusa, "Diplomacy in the Age of Globalization."

ॐ

Harvard Program on Humanitarian Policy and Conflict Research. "Bibliography on Human Security." August 2001 (available from [http://www.hpcrresearch.org/publications/other-publications]; accessed 22 February 2010).

Although dated, this 24-page paper remains an important resource for research on "human security." The bibliography includes "books, chapters in books, journal and magazine articles, scholarly papers, manuscripts, speeches, presentations, reports, and government publications, including official statements, political agreements, and press releases" (p. 2). The inclusion of William Ernest Blatz's *Human Security: Some Reflections* (London: University of London Press), published in 1967, is a reminder that the idea—indeed the very name—of human security has been in play for decades.

↝

Human Security Centre. *Human Security Report 2005: War and Peace in the 21st Century.* New York: Oxford University Press, 2005 (available from [http://www.hsrgroup.org/human-security-reports/2005/overview.aspx]; accessed 27 August 2009).

Affiliated with the Human Security Report Project, which at the time of publication was a component of the Human Security Centre at the University of British Columbia, the authors of this report analyze existing and newly generated datasets and conclude that wars, civil conflicts, genocides, and other crises involving large-scale human rights violations dramatically declined from peak levels witnessed in the 1990s. The report credits this positive trend, in large measure, to conflict reduction efforts spearheaded by the United Nations and other key international actors.

Of particular interest to readers of this bibliography is the *Report*'s one-page discussion entitled "What is Human Security?" (p. VIII), which is summarized here. "Human security" is defined as protection against direct physical threats generated by violent conflicts such as wars and genocides. A new doctrine of security, human security, is needed because established measures for securing states against external attack are rarely effective in preventing the types of conflicts that occur within sovereign borders.

Although all adherents of the human security model focus on safeguarding individuals, the *Report* discerns the existence of two approaches to the concept. The "narrow" school of human security concentrates on preventing or ameliorating dangers posed by violence, while the "broad" interpretation of human security is concerned with threats like food shortages, lack of healthcare, and environmental calamities. A yet broader interpretation of human security seeks to bolster peoples' economic wellbeing and "dignity."

Although it asserts that the two conceptions of human security cohere rather than conflict, the *Report* adopts the narrow, violence-prevention definition, for two reasons: first, several other research reports on the state of the world analyze the factors covered by the broad definition of human security; and second, the narrow understanding enjoys greater traction within policymaking circles, which increasingly appreciate "the interrelatedness of security, development and the protection of civilians."

Three follow-on publications to the *Human Security Report 2005* have been produced: *Human Security Brief 2006*, *Human Security Brief 2007*, and *Human Security Report 2009/2010* (all are available from [http://www.hsrgroup.org/human-security-reports/human-security-report.aspx]).

❧

Hussein, Karim, Donata Gnisci, and Julia Wanjiru. "Security and Human Security: An Overview of Concepts and Initiatives—What Implications for West Africa?" SWAC Issue Paper. Paris: Sahel and West Africa Club (SWAC), December 2004 (available from [http://www.oecd.org/dataoecd/32/2/38826090.pdf]; accessed 1 August 2009).

Prepared under the auspices of the Sahel and West Africa Club (SWAC), a regionally focused research and advocacy division of the Organisation for Economic Co-operation and Development (OECD), this 47-page study is especially noteworthy because it provides an assessment of "human security" tailored for an African readership (for another source that engages human security from the perspective of the "developing" world, see the entry in this bibliography for United Nations Development Programme, *Arab Human Development Report 2009*). A central goal of the paper, therefore, is to acquaint SWAC members and affiliates with the ideas, vocabulary, and practices of human security in order to spur debate on the concept and how it can be calibrated to address West African realities.

The authors usefully identify a continuing challenge for the student and practitioner of human security, namely the lack of a harmonized definition of the term. Human security, they write, entails the safety of individuals not merely in a physical sense, but also in terms of their political, economic, and social status. Human security is a widely accepted component of international development, yet

"[d]espite the consensus on the foundations of this concept, *an uncontroversial definition of human security does not currently exist.* Since the mid 1990s, the UN Commission for Human Security, the UNDP, the World Bank, the OECD Development Assistance Committee and the national governments of Japan, United Kingdom, Canada, and others have worked to identify its key components. Nonetheless, *definitions continue to be broad,* emphasising the protection of human beings and local communities from a variety of threats, ranging from individual to collective, and from physical to political, economic, social, or environmental" (p. 8, emphasis added).

With crisply written text and informative sidebars, figures, and bibliography, this SWAC paper is more than a resource for West Africans; it is of value to all those seeking insight into the complications and possibilities of human security. In this regard, the report's fourth section—entitled "Issues Raised and Key Questions for the Region"—is particularly useful thanks to the inclusion of a series of thought-provoking queries. The sub-section called "Translate the concept of human security into practice," for example, features questions relevant to all regions of the globe, such as "Whose responsibility is it to guarantee human security...? What are the specific roles of states, non-state and regional actors?" (p. 31).

༄

Lavrov, Sergey V. "A Conversation with Sergey Lavrov." Interview by David Remnick at the Council on Foreign Relations in New York, 24 September 2008 (transcript available from [http://www.cfr.org/un/conversation-sergey-lavrov/p17384]; accessed 28 August 2010).

In the course of this interview, Russian Foreign Minister Sergey Lavrov issues a pointed defense of his country's decision to use military force against its neighbor, Georgia, in August of 2008. Reviewing the details of the Russia-Georgia war is beyond the scope of this bibliography,[39] but relevant is Lavrov's reference to the United Nations Charter and two UN-sponsored humanitarian doctrines:

"...Russian action to stop the aggression of Georgia against South Ossetia, the action [was] firmly rooted in the right for self-defense as enshrined in Article 51 of the charter....So we could not—we could not tolerate this. And if all this talk about *responsibility to protect* is going to remain just talk, if all this talk about *human security* is going to be used only to initiate some pathetic debate in the United Nations and elsewhere, then we believe this is wrong. So *we exercised the human security maxim, we exercised the responsibility to protect*..." (emphasis added).

The Russian foreign minister's statement reveals a reality of international relations: major powers invoke humanitarian doctrines to justify unilateral military intervention. As "human security" is established as an operational concept, inevitably certain countries will exploit it as a diplomatic weapon and rationalization for military action. Historically, both Hitler and Stalin appealed to self-determination and the protection of minorities as justifications for invading foreign countries.

Because human security is built on a foundation of ideals, it is susceptible to cooptation. As the Israeli statesman Abba Eban observed: "My experience tells me that all governments take their decisions in the name of self interest and then explain their

---

[39] For an account that is critical of Russia's behavior, see Ronald D. Asmus, *A Little War That Shook the World: Georgia, Russia, and the Future of the West* (New York: Palgrave Macmillan, 2010). Asmus served as deputy assistant secretary of state for European affairs under U.S. President Bill Clinton.

decisions in the name of morality."[40] Distortion of human security might also occur if the concept becomes too closely aligned with military strategy and tactics. In his book *The Accidental Guerrilla*, David Kilcullen argues that

"Effective counterinsurgency provides human security to the population, where they live, 24 hours a day. This, not destroying the enemy, is the central task."[41]

The dangers of allowing human security to become too closely aligned with military operations must be anticipated and debated.

⌇

Miliband, David. "Better World, Better Britain." Speech before the annual Foreign and Commonwealth Office Leadership Conference, Queen Elizabeth II Conference Centre in London, 4 March 2008 (available from [http://www.fco.gov.uk/]; accessed 5 March 2008).

David Miliband served as Britain's foreign secretary from 2007 to 2010, and in that capacity he delivered this speech wherein he shares some remarkable reflections on international relations. For example, both proponents and opponents of the Westphalian world order composed of nation-states enjoying inviolable rights will be intrigued by Miliband's frank admission that "[w]e cling to the notion of sovereignty, yet all the time we are interfering in each other's affairs." For the then foreign secretary, advancing "human security"—a term he does not define in this address—justifies overriding the old Westphalian imperatives:

"...power is moving upwards to continental and global institutions, from formal institutions like the EU, WTO and UN, to informal institutions that govern the internet. This partly reflects....changing values and *the primacy we place on human security and human freedom over traditional notions of sovereignty*" (emphasis added).

---

[40] Abba Eban, "Prospects for Peace in the Middle East," the Annual David Davies Memorial Lecture delivered on 26 October 1988 (London: The David Davies Memorial Institute of International Studies, n.d.), 10.

[41] David Kilcullen, *The Accidental Guerrilla: Small Wars in the Midst of a Big One* (New York: Oxford University Press, 2009), 266.

If human security is to be transformed from notional concept to operative policies amid a world in which sovereign states remain the primary actors, then national policymakers must provide the leadership to move in that direction. In particular, guidance by major powers like Britain, one of the five permanent members of the UN Security Council, is crucial.

During the 1965 *Pacem in Terris* ("peace on earth") conference held in New York City, the diplomat Abba Eban proposed "for discussion that the heads of all sovereign governments, within and outside the UN, devote a week of their time to consider the problems not of any nation but of the human nation."[42] Four years before Eban spoke, the American diplomat (and former presidential candidate) Adlai Stevenson suggested holding "an occasional seminar for statesmen" where "they could be induced to divorce themselves for even a few days from the griminess of daily politics" and, instead, explore higher issues like ethics and values. Such a leadership seminar, Stevenson asserted, would help participants be "much better leaders for the rest of the year."[43]

Although at the time listeners may have dismissed their words as windy rhetoric, in today's era of intensified globalization the proposals of Eban and Stevenson are more realistic and necessary. In fact, the increasing frequency and importance of multilateral diplomacy—both at the working and senior levels—suggests that a new global leadership corps might be emerging, albeit by default rather than design. With encouragement and perhaps specialized training, leaders in politics and diplomacy could be empowered to think about, and respond to, the dictates of "world interest" even as they pursue an established pattern defined by "national interest." Only in such an environment will human security, however defined, thrive.

$\backsim$

---

[42] Quoted in Edward Reed, ed., *Peace on Earth—Pacem in Terris* (New York: Pocket Books, 1965), 45. *Pacem in Terris* was the title of an encyclical on peace issued by Pope John XXIII in April 1963.

[43] Adlai Stevenson, "An Ethic for Survival," speech delivered in New York City on 23 May 1961, in *An Ethic For Survival: Adlai Stevenson Speaks on International Affairs, 1936-1965*, eds. Michael H. Prosser and Lawrence H. Sherlick (New York: William Morrow and Company, Inc., 1969), 312. At the time of this speech, Stevenson was the U.S. ambassador to the United Nations.

Ministry of Foreign Affairs of Japan. "The Trust Fund for Human Security: For the 'Human-centered' 21st Century." Tokyo: Ministry of Foreign Affairs of Japan, 2007.

Admirably concise at nine pages plus Appendix, this statement provides an official Japanese perspective on "human security." As such, it is analogous to the Canadian government's paper entitled "Freedom from Fear."[44] Unlike Canada, however, Japan favors a definition of the concept that is consistent with a "broad" interpretation[45] of human security:

"Human security aims to protect people from critical and pervasive threats to human lives, livelihoods and dignity, and thus to enhance human fulfillment. For these objectives, human security tries to integrate and strengthen initiatives that emphasize human-centered perspectives" (p. 2).

After describing what human security is, the Japanese statement usefully traces the history of efforts by the United Nations, UN member states (including Japan), and nongovernmental organizations to define and institutionalize human security as a major theme of international relations. The second section of the document sketches Japan's own human security initiatives, while the third part illustrates the operations and budget of the UN's Trust Fund for Human Security, of which Japan is a major funder.

Beyond documenting the specifics of Japan's commitment to human security, this document is significant for two additional reasons. First, it spotlights the pattern of post-World War II Japanese foreign relations, which is a deliberate and dramatic break from that country's previous record of aggressive nationalism and militarism. Second, it demonstrates how a middle-ranking power like Japan can make significant contributions to international relations by promoting innovative policies, in this case a novel approach to security (human security). In this way Japan and its peers like Canada (which not coincidentally is also a second-tier

---

[44] See above, alphabetized under Department of Foreign Affairs and International Trade.

[45] For a brief discussion of the "narrow" and "broad" interpretations of human security, see the entry in this bibliography for Human Security Centre, *Human Security Report 2005: War and Peace in the 21st Century.*

power)[46] are helping the world to glimpse the outlines of, in the words of this report, a "'Human-centered' 21st Century."

جۍ

Rothschild, Emma. "What is Security?" *Daedalus* 124 (Summer 1995): 53-98.

This essay is included in a special issue of the journal *Daedalus* devoted to the theme, "The Quest for World Order." Rothschild assesses "human security"—also called "common security" or "extended security"—from the perspective of post-Cold War international relations and the new (or old) directions they might take. The timing of this essay's publication (in 1995) is notable because it was six years after the fall of the Berlin Wall (in 1989) and six years before the fall of New York's Twin Towers (in 2001), both of which entailed consequences that profoundly altered global politics. In terms of the debate on the nature of security, 1989 seemed to promise new possibilities while 2001 at least temporarily provoked a reversion to traditional policies. Rothschild, of course, was focused on what had happened, not what would occur.

Rothschild states that the Cold War was an international conflict. Like other wars—those of the Napoleonic era and the two world wars of the twentieth century—when it ended the question was posed: "What principles of security will now prevail?" According to Rothschild, although the post-Cold War era has no Woodrow Wilson to articulate authoritative principles, it does have an emerging idea in the form of human security. The case against human security, as presented by Rothschild, is as follows: the principles that underpin it (like the security of individuals) are not new, they cannot be captured in inspiring slogans (such as Wilson's "self-determination"), and there is no international organization (like the UN) specifically charged with upholding them.

---

[46] See Ronald M. Behringer, "Middle Power Leadership on the Human Security Agenda," *Cooperation and Conflict* 40 (September 2005): 305-342.

In his book *Diplomacy: A Very Short Introduction* (New York: Oxford University Press, 2010), the scholar Joseph Siracusa writes: "Human security was presaged in the policies of small to medium powers" (p. 114). For further discussion of Siracusa's book, see the relevant bibliography entry below.

On the other hand, argues Rothschild, human security has features that recommend it to the post-Cold War environment. Human security's very amorphousness, for example, gives it a flexibility needed to meet the challenges of a fluid, post-bipolar international order. In fact, guidance on formulating principles of security can be obtained in the writings of eighteenth-century European philosophers, who confronted a pluralistic international system not unlike that of the late twentieth century. Thinkers such as Immanuel Kant and Adam Smith, asserts Rothschild, were concerned with the security of states *and* the security of individuals. They—like modern advocates of human security—were keen to link the two: secure states meant secure individuals, and vice versa.

ᴈꙮ

Siracusa, Joseph M. "Diplomacy in the Age of Globalization." In *Diplomacy: A Very Short Introduction.* New York: Oxford University Press, 2010.

This chapter is included in a book by the historian Joseph Siracusa which is part of the Oxford University Press series called Very Short Introductions (VSI). Commensurate with VSI's abbreviated format, Siracusa's treatment of "human security" is brief but, nevertheless, erudite and thought-provoking. He implicitly endorses a "broad" interpretation[47] of the concept by noting that threats to human security are by definition "polymorphous" (p. 107), meaning one type of threat (e.g., violent conflict) can provoke a multitude of subsequent perils (e.g., economic disruption, human rights violations, and degradation of health services). "To define a security crisis as military, environmental, societal, or financial," Siracusa writes, "is to downplay the 'strings' or 'threads' of interconnected happenings, decisions, ideas, and beliefs that shape trajectories of risk" (pp. 107-8).

Significantly, when Siracusa later returns to the question of how to define human security, he argues that a viable definition should serve the world of thought (scholarship), the world of

---

[47] See note 45 and the text corresponding thereto.

action (policymaking), and the wider world's need for a realistic framework of order:

"For a definition of human security to have explanatory force, and to appeal to decision-maker and researchers alike, it must establish a conceptual link with notions of world order. To put it another way, decision-makers need the intellectual equipment and disposition to see the 'full spectrum' of security to identify security risks and preventive measures that do not escalate into the use of force. Further, to be serviceable at a policy level, such a definition must be anchored to a realization of the limitations imposed by an imperfect 'anarchic' inter-state system" (p. 113).

Another book in Oxford's VSI series, Finnish scholar Jussi Hanhimäki's *The United Nations: A Very Short Introduction* (New York: Oxford University Press, 2008), touches on human security (see the chapter section entitled "Human security and the 'responsibility to protect' [pp. 125-27]). Treating human security in the context of the evolution of the United Nations, Hanhimäki notes that by the time usage of the phrase became widespread, the UN system already featured a constellation of agencies dealing with human security-type issues, including UNDP, FAO, ILO, IFAD, UNESCO, UNICEF, WHO, and UNEP. "To a large extent," concludes Hanhimäki, "'human security' was but a new collective noun to explain what the UN was already doing" (p. 126).

ॐ

UNESCO. *What Agenda for Human Security in the Twenty-first Century?*, 2d ed. Proceedings of the First International Meeting of Directors of Peace Research and Training Institutions convened on 27-28 November 2000. Paris: UNESCO, 2005.

The enduring value of this collection of conference papers is reflected in the fact that it was originally published in 2001 and later released as a second edition in revised format four years later (the subsequent version is reviewed here). The compilation features an admirable diversity of geographical/cultural viewpoints; an unfortunate and glaring exception to this rule is the almost total absence of participants and perspectives from the United States[48] (this phenomenon is ongoing: the general U.S. disregard for the concept and practice of "human security" is a recurring topic in the Interactive Dialogue published above).

Proceedings as wide-ranging as these defy easy summarization. What can be said in a brief appreciation is that a careful reading reveals a twin, unifying theme: within the thought, rhetoric, and practice of international relations, the broad meaning of *security* is evolving and the specific significance of *human security* is emerging.

On the changing nature of security in general, see especially Bjørn Møller's contribution on "National, Societal and Human Security" (pp. 77-127). His Table entitled "Expanded concepts of 'security'" (p. 87) provides an excellent graphical representation of the current state of play of security as a shifting concept (see above Appendix 4, "Some Representations of Human Security," for a reproduction). Also noteworthy are Philippe Ratte's comments on the fading viability of the classic security framework based on the territorial state (pp. 75-76).

Regarding the significance of human security, the starting point of such an evaluation is the existence of a viable and accepted definition of term. In his Keynote Address to the conference, entitled "Towards human security" (and revealingly subtitled "a people-centred approach to foreign policy"), the Canadian diplomat Louis Hamel asserts that "[h]uman security is simply defined: it means freedom from pervasive threats to the rights, the safety, or the lives of people" (p. 29).

Unfortunately for its proponents and potential beneficiaries, the meaning of human security has been deceptively simple in that it has been easy to explain in theory but difficult to implement in practice. It is telling that a decade after it was first drafted, the following conclusion contained in the conference's "Final Recommendations" remains valid: "Human security can be considered today as a paradigm in the making..." (p. 225). Indeed,

---

[48] Of the 108 persons included in the "List of Participants" on pp. 249-63, *only one* is affiliated with an institution located in the United States (Carolyn Stephenson of the University of Hawaii at Manoa).

according to Jamil Ahsan human security has been in the making not for years or decades, but centuries; he traces the concept back to the early 1700s and the writings of the philosopher Gottfried Leibniz (p. 203).

ぷ

United Nations Development Programme. *Human Development Report 1994*. New York: Oxford University Press, 1994 (available from [http://hdr.undp.org/en/reports/global/hdr1994/]; accessed 27 August 2009).

When tracing the origins of an influential idea, it is often necessary to move further and further back in history because a decisive moment of revelation cannot be determined. For its part, "human security" may not lack such moment in that this document can reasonably be credited as its foundational statement. According to the Japanese foreign ministry, "[t]he 1994 'Human Development Report' by the United Nations Development Programme (UNDP) was the first to mention human security publicly in the international community."[49] Because the UNDP *Report* has been, and continues to be, cited and discussed throughout the literature on human security, its definition of that term carries special importance:

"Human security can be said to have two main aspects. It means, first, safety from such chronic threats as hunger, disease and repression. And second, it means protection from sudden and hurtful disruptions in the patterns of daily life—whether in homes, in jobs or in communities" (p. 23).

In subsequent years a debate about "narrow" and "broad" interpretations of human security emerged,[50] but the UNDP clearly champions a vision of human security that is wide-ranging as well as preventive:[51]

---

[49] Ministry of Foreign Affairs of Japan, "The Trust Fund for Human Security: For the 'Human-centered' 21st Century" (Tokyo: Ministry of Foreign Affairs of Japan, 2007), 2. For further discussion of the foreign ministry's paper, see the appropriate bibliography entry above.

[50] See note 47 and especially note 45 together with text corresponding to both.

[51] On human security as a preventive approach, see note 38 and the text corresponding thereto.

"In the final analysis, human security is a child who did not die, a disease that did not spread, a job that was not cut, an ethnic tension that did not explode in violence, a dissident who was not silenced. Human security is not a concern with weapons—it is a concern with human life and dignity" (p. 22).

Boldly predicting that the concept "is likely to revolutionize society in the 21st century" (p. 22), the UNDP *Report* outlines a model of human security with four defining features: universality (human security is of concern to peoples in all countries and at every socio-economic level); interdependence (threats occurring in one country or region inevitably affect the wider world community); prevention (which is more effective and inexpensive than reacting to threats after they become acute); and a focus on the wellbeing of individuals (rather than nation-states).

In addition to laying the conceptual foundations of human security—in ways that continue to guide scholars and practitioners—the *Human Development Report 1994* contains numerous Tables and Figures that illuminate key topics, such as global spending on military forces versus anti-poverty programs. Although the *Report's* data are dated, the broad patterns and implications they reveal remain valid and thought-provoking (for an example, see above, Appendix 4 "Some Representations of Human Security", Figure 10 "The human cost of military spending in developing countries").

جرٌ

United Nations Development Programme. *Arab Human Development Report 2009: Challenges to Human Security in the Arab Countries.* New York: United Nations Development Programme, 2009 (available from [http://www.arab-hdr.org/contents/index. aspx?rid=5]; accessed 10 August 2010).

This comprehensive analysis is part of a landmark series produced by the United Nations Development Programme. Inaugurated with the release of the *Arab Human Development Report 2002: Creating Opportunities for Future Generations*, these studies have been released during a critical decade in Arab and world history (in

2002, 2003, 2004, 2005, and 2009). The first report, for example, was published in the wake of the 11 September 2001 terrorist attacks and the second amidst the US-led occupation of Iraq. In a sense, then, the 2002 and 2003 reports can be interpreted as responses to those historic events. Both studies describe the background conditions—including gross deficiencies in free speech, access to education, and social tolerance—which help nurture instability, including the phenomenon of terrorists who claim the sanction of religion. Furthermore, having been written during the build-up, invasion, and early occupation phases of the Iraq war, the development report for 2003 presents the case for internal change from within the Arab world. This option for internal change is contrasted with the US-led occupation of Iraq, which is described as an effort to impose change externally.

As indicated by its subtitle, the *Arab Human Development Report 2009* focuses on issues of "human security" in an Arab context. In its discussion of the conceptual issues surrounding human security—the essential starting point of any such investigation—the *Report* defines it in relation to human development and human rights:

"Human security is the 'rearguard of human development'. Whereas human development is concerned with expanding the individual's capabilities and opportunities, human security focuses on enabling peoples to contain or avert threats to their lives, livelihoods and human dignity. The two concepts look at the human condition from different ends of a continuum....The intellectual frameworks they provide are co-extensive and mutually reinforcing. Moreover, human security is related to human rights inasmuch as respect for people's basic rights creates conditions favourable to human security" (p. 2).

A major theme of the *Arab Human Development Report 2009* is the necessity for the Arab world to transcend its "received" notion of security, meaning the prioritization of state security to the exclusion of other essential concerns, including the wellbeing of individuals. In a letter to the editor published in the *New York Times*, Ann Kerr asserts that Arabs have experienced "a century of frustration" which she attributes, in part, to "their mostly unsuccessful attempts to build their own national governments."[52] In the view of the *Arab Human Development Report 2009*, Arab state-building has failed precisely because Arab governments have willfully denied, or been unable to provide, human security for their populations. In the words of UN official Amat Al Alim Alsoswa, "in the long run, the government that pursues state security without investing in human security is the government that achieves neither" (p. VI).

It is to be hoped that the next Arab Human Development Report will analyze the "Arab Spring" movements which, as of this writing, have ousted authoritarian leaders in Tunisia and Egypt and shacken other Arab ruling circles at their foundations. Optimistically, the new patterns of governance that may emerge in at least some Arab countries will find inspiration in the pages of the *Arab Human Development Report 2009* and its predecessors.

ॐ

United Nations General Assembly. "2005 World Summit Outcome." 15 September 2005 (available from [http://www.un.org/summit2005/documents.html]; accessed 27 August 2010).

"Human security" hardly constitutes a major theme of this United Nations General Assembly statement; in fact, the concept is relegated one brief paragraph as the 143rd of 178 points. Nevertheless, the document places the General Assembly on record as supporting human security:

"We stress the right of people to live in freedom and dignity, free from poverty and despair. We recognize that all individuals, in particular vulnerable people, are entitled to freedom from fear and freedom from want, with an equal opportunity to enjoy all their rights and fully develop their human potential. To this end, we commit ourselves to discussing and defining the notion of human security in the General Assembly" (p. 32).

---

[52] Ann Kerr, "Terrorism in Lebanon," letter to the editor, *New York Times*, 2 November 2008 (available from [http://www.nytimes.com/2008/11/02/opinion/lweb02lebanon.html]; accessed 2 November 2008). Kerr is the widow of Malcolm H. Kerr, the president of the American Universtiy of Beirut who in 1984 was shot to death outside his office by gunmen. At the time, Lebanon was in the midst of a protracted civil war which did not end until 1990.

Advocates of the human security approach have reason to be disappointed with this "World Summit Outcome." More than a decade after the United Nations Development Programme issued a comprehensive study and endorsement of human security in its *Human Development Report 1994* (see bibliography entry above), the General Assembly could only "stress" the value of the concept; its statement does not commit the UN to any concrete policies and promises merely to discuss and define the "notion"—not model, doctrine, or principle—of human security.

Today, the promise of internationally accepted standards of human security remains just that: a promise yet to be fulfilled. Even in the more urgent area of international humanitarian intervention to end gross human rights violations—in UN jargon, the "responsibility to protect"—which is also mentioned in the 2005 General Assembly statement, the international community must still rely on a single tool: armed intervention by a major power or coalition of powers. The NATO intervention in Libya initiated in March 2011 demonstrates that years after the Kosovo and Iraq interventions, the international community has two basic options when faced with large-scale human rights violations: acquiesce or bomb.

United States Agency for International Development. "Human Security and USAID." Note drafted by the Bureau for Policy and Program Coordination on 21 December 2000; rev. on 4 January 2001 (copy in the possession of J. A. Grayzel).

For the text of this document—as well as a brief introductory note explaining its significance—see above, Appendix 5, "Human Security and the United States Agency for International Development."

The World Bank and the Human Security Report Project. *miniAtlas of Human Security*. Brighton, UK: Myriad Editions, 2008.

This compact (in size and length) reference book presents a series of informative maps, charts, and graphs—together with concise explanatory text—in a glossy, easy-to-digest format. The information is grouped into five parts, each with two or three subsections: "When States Go to War," "Warlords and Killing Fields," "Counting the Dead," "Measuring Human Rights Abuse," and "Causes of War, Causes of Peace." Printed on the inside front cover and first page of the *miniAtlas* is a brief, instructive treatment of "human security" which includes discussion of its relationship with national security as well as an examination of the "narrow" and "broad" interpretations[53] of the concept.

---

[53] See notes 50, 47, and especially note 45 together with text corresponding to all three.